FIRST STEPS
TO FLY FISHING

The 1924 Classic Updated for Today

Written by

Michael Temple & Kris Neely

Introduction by Fly Fishing Expert Joshua Bergan

A Huckleberry Imprint

CRESTINGWAVE
PUBLISHING

ISBN: 978-0-9889048-9-7

A **Huckleberry** imprint from **Cresting Wave Publishing**, LLC
Published by Cresting Wave Publishing, LLC.

"You buy a book. We plant a tree."

Cover design: Kris and Laura Neely
Interior Book Design: Lazar Kackarovski

Stock photography: www.shutterstock.com

Table of Contents

Figure 1 *Published March 1, 1817 by S&J Fuller, London, England.*

Dedication

To Michael Temple.

Godspeed, sir.
Your fine work lives again
for another generation to profit from.

To my son Parker Kristopher Neely.
In hopes, he will, one day, master the joys of fly fishing.

Kris Neely
Summer, 2020
Merced, California

Editor's Comments

I MAGINE YOU BOUGHT AN antique dining room table and chairs. Built in, say, 1924. Let's stipulate that they *seem* to be in mostly decent shape. But think of what you could do to really tune that fantastic set of furniture with:

- contemporary wood polishes
- modern scratch concealers
- current upholstery cleaners
- modern memory foam seats
- super glue
- tightly engineered screws and fasteners

The list goes on, but the result would be the same: an even better masterpiece of the furniture maker's art, incorporating some of the past and some of the future.

The point would not be to build a whole new dining set. It would be to integrate helpful tools, techniques, and knowledge from today with the woodworker's art of a century ago. If "seams" showed between "yesterday" and "today," so much the better.

Now take that idea and substitute a masterpiece of writing called *First Steps to Fly Fishing* by Michael Temple for the table and chairs. And take a professional fly fisher and author like Joshua Bergan to supply today's critical expert's eye. Mix in some of today's techniques, technology, and knowledge, and the result would be the book you are now reading.

That was the goal that Cresting Wave Publishing set our sights on—melding the expert instruction of a century ago (when people often had quite literally to fish for their supper) with today's science, tech, and experience.

Yes—a discerning reader can and will detect some of the "seams" between Mr. Temple's writing, Mr. Bergan's, and mine. But these new/old parts make up a better whole: a book from the 1920s for the 2020s. And beyond.

Here then is *First Steps to Fly Fishing*—and thank you for joining us on this literary adventure.

Sincerely,

Kris Neely

Publisher / Cresting Wave Publishing

"You buy a book. We plant a tree."

Introduction to the New 21st Century Edition

by Joshua Bergan

"The sport and game of angling are the true means and cause that brings a man into a merry spirit, which makes a flowering age and a long one."
~ Dame Juliana Berners ~

MOST WOULD AGREE THAT learning to fly fish can be an intimidating journey to embark upon. Aside from getting the dedicated help of an avid fly-fishing friend or family member or paying a month's wages to a fly shop or outfitter, beginners don't have many options for shortcuts to competence and success. Most, including Dame Juliana, would also agree that it is worth the effort.

Fly fishing is largely timeless. The idea of fooling fish with flies, line, and rod hasn't evolved quickly. The gear, language, and attitudes may have come of age, but the fundamental building blocks (or 'first steps' if you will) haven't changed, which is why Michael Temple's 1924 book, *First Steps to Fly Fishing,* is being re-released by Cresting Wave Publishing.

First Steps to Fly Fishing is one of the earliest texts devoted to acquainting neophytes with the basics of fly fishing. Temple's eloquent words have held up well.

Temple's overarching strategy is to *keep it simple,* with minimal monetary investment. Says Temple:

> *There is no need to fit yourself out with all the newest and most expensive gadgets, and I am going to try to keep your expenditure on tackle as low as I can.*
>
> *It is not necessary to have much, but what you have must be reliable and durable. It is often possible to pick up bargains at estate, garage, and yard sales. Failing that, shop a tackle maker with an established reputation and put yourself in their hands.*

Choosing what topics need to be covered in an intro to fly fishing textbook can be a challenge, but Temple, with a bit of modernization from Cresting Wave, has done a nice job. There are updated sections on rods, reels, lines, and other equipment, loads of information on specific recommended flies, how to cast, where to fish, when to fish, and more. And don't discount the value of a fly angler's glossary, which is included as the final section of this book. Temple thoughtfully omits more advanced concepts, such as fly tying, line mending, and entomology (with brief exceptions in the "Flies" section). Reading *First Steps to Fly Fishing* is quick, easy, to the point, and won't leave your head spinning.

Be aware that, while it does give some coverage to hatches, this book does not cover regional hatch variations. Temple speaks of the "sulphur" hatch, which is an insect found in Europe and the eastern U.S. but does not occur in the American West. Likewise, he states that green and gray drakes are the same species with color variations—this is not the case for today's American anglers; they are distinct species of mayflies. Don't put too much faith in Temple's hatch timing either, as hatches are area-based, and he was from across the pond. But do understand that fishing any specific hatch requires planning and good timing.

Being that the author was from England and that this text was written nearly 100 years ago, some the vernacular is noticeably of the day ("bloa" and "watchet," for example). In the section on learning to cast, Temple says, "Have you a lawn? Capital!" Got to love the British. There are also lots of "shalls" and "certainlies" which paint a picture of a pleasant grandfatherly lecture.

Where his actual advice might show its age a bit, Cresting Wave has inserted modern takes. In the "Flies" section, an updated 21st Century list of recommended flies accompanies the author's original 1924 list, which is good, because most fly shop employees would look at you funny if you asked for a "Dotterel" or "Coch-y-Bonddu," as Temple advocated. Inquiring about a Woolly Bugger, Copper John, or Gold-ribbed Hare's Ear will yield much better results in the shop, and maybe the river as well.

The new publisher has also added input from modern websites and anglers, such as advice on fishing terrestrials from the Orvis Company, and guidance on how to fish a specific hatch from the team at *www. guiderecommended.com.*

Remarkably, much of the information on rods and reels has withstood the test of time. For example, in the "Rods" section, Temple states:

> *In terms of length, seven to ten feet is quite long enough. Another option: get a four- or five-weight rod. These are quite versatile and are suitable for a variety of targets from trout to bass. Fly rod manufacturers today sell the majority of their rods in 9-foot lengths.*

This is as true today as it was then.

Likewise, his recommendation on including a "priest" (a bat used for quickly dispatching fish bound for the fryer) might seem passé, and likely would have been a decade or two ago. But a current shift in attitude about the ethics of keeping a fish here and there has brought the priest back into necessary fashion.

With a little luck, this edition will be around long enough to become a classic again.

As Temple acknowledges, this book is geared toward traditional fly fishing for trout. While the sport has expanded and become an effective means for catching saltwater species, warm water quarry, and anything else that swims, covering all the types of fly fishing is not the job of a book that aims to initiate people to the sport.

There is not much information available on author Michael Temple. We know he was an English writer and that the original 1924 edition of this book was printed by British publisher Mills and Boon – which, entirely unrelatedly I'm sure, has since transitioned to publishing... romantic fiction.

We can surmise that the original publication of *First Steps to Fly Fishing* was a significant achievement, as, at that time, the publisher was generating other successful titles including many by famous outdoorsman and author Jack London. Temple had previously authored at least one other book, a novel entitled *Shallowdale: Ourselves, Our Friends, and Our Village*.

Ultimately, when it comes to the subject of this book, it is clearly and almost touchingly evident that Temple gets it. And that he shared the same love for fly fishing that so many of us have today. He says:

> *If you are the pure fly fisher breed, you will have many days at the end of which you will come home with an empty creel and yet be able to say quite honestly that you have had an excellent day of sport fishing.*
>
> *To the person who loves fly fishing, there is no sport in the world to which it compares.*

That passion hasn't changed, and the sport shows no signs of losing followers. Especially in this age of anxiety, electronics, and constant scrolling on cell phones, it would likely benefit many people to get back to nature in pursuit of trout by way of the fly rod. And, of course, a few more passionate anglers and clean-water defenders are always welcome.

Fly fishing is undoubtedly complicated, which can be one of the most significant obstacles and intimidating factors facing prospective fly fishers. If you've always wanted to serenely cast a picturesque fly to the beautiful creature known as a trout but don't have an acquaintance to hold your hand through the complicated lingo, techniques, and science of fly fishing, this book will be your new best friend.

Good luck!

Joshua Bergan, Summer 2020

A Very Brief History of Fly Fishing

(21st Century)

FLY FISHING HAS ENDURED for hundreds, possibly thousands, of years as one of the most challenging, artistic, and aesthetic forms of bringing fish to hand. From beginnings rooted in the practical and throughout its storied timeline, fly fishing has been many things to many anglers and continues to be a high-profile pastime worldwide.

200 B.C. –1500 A.D.

While there are some unverified depictions of fly fishing dating back to the years B.C. in both Japan and Egypt, the first credible account of fly fishing comes from the Roman writer Claudius Aelianus in his work, *On the Nature of Animals* (*De Natura Animalium*) around 200 A.D.

Said Aelianus: "...when the fish observes a fly on the surface, it swims quietly up, afraid to stir the water above lest it should scare away its prey; then coming up by its shadow, it opens its mouth gently and gulps down the fly..."

In these early days, fishing with flies was done without a rod, in a process known as "hand lining." However, some artwork suggests rods have been used for other types of fishing since B.C.

Anglers soon began using short twigs as rods, and later long sticks with a dedicated line tied to the top. At this time, fishing lines were crafted of tied-together sections of horse (yes, the animal) tail hair (which had roughly a one-pound-test strength). The flies were made of wool, fur, and feathers tied onto what were called "gorges," which were primitive hooks made of bone, wood, or later, bent needles. The use of reels, though possibly introduced in China around 300 A.D., was not a common practice at the time.

We can surmise that fly fishing had been going on for some time before Aelianus's early writings, but the exact dates are not precise. Over the next several hundred years, few reports seem to point to fly fishing (or more likely few accounts survived). However, the sport—and essential source of sustenance—no doubt continued to evolve.

We know this in part because in 1496, the first thorough chronicle of fly fishing, titled *A Treatyse of Fysshynge wyth an Angle,* was penned by an English nun named Dame Juliana Berners.

The treatise told of techniques, rods, lines, flies, and tips that still work today. Included are instructions on how to craft a fly rod from specific woods and processes, how to make a horsehair fly line, and how to craft hooks from needles—all of which were time-consuming endeavors.

Her book is still available to read online. (Fair warning! Ye Olde English can be a bit tricky to decipher.)

1500-1800

By the year 1500, aided by Berners's tome and Johannes Gutenberg's invention of the printing press, fly fishing gained popularity, and written/printed accounts of the sport rose dramatically.

Books such as *The Secrets of Angling* by John Dennys (a companion of William Shakespeare) boosted the collective knowledge. Soon, anglers were able to build on each other's findings quicker and with more reach than before.

In 1653, *The Compleat Angler*, by Sir Izaak Walton, was published and is easily the most widely distributed and most influential fishing book in history (in fact, it is reportedly one of the most printed manuals in the history of the world). *The Compleat Angler* covered fishing tackle, bait, fish species, habitat, cooking fish, and more. It was not until a revision of the book in 1676 that fly fishing was introduced into *The Compleat Angler*, via a contribution by Charles Cotton.

Being that most of this era's fly fishing literature was written in English, the sport's gains were mostly limited to Northern Europe. Similar styles of fishing with flies were, however, coincidentally occurring in other parts of the world, such as Japan.

Tales of Japanese "tenkara" fishing (a form of fishing with flies tied to fixed-length lines attached to the tips of rods without reels, similar to the European style) date back to the 1600s. However, the first formal records on tenkara came from Englishmen in the 1870s. Interestingly, tenkara fishing is currently seeing a resurgence in popularity worldwide.

Fly rods soon lengthened to over 15 feet. Eventually, the innovation of rod guides made it possible to use longer lines, which aided in reaching and fighting for and against farther away fish. The rod guides (also known as rod rings) spread the weight/force/tension/energy (involved when a fish is attached to one end of a taut fishing line) across the entire length and breadth of the fishing rod. This had an additional side benefit: it helped rods last longer.

Additionally, anglers started using specialized rods for different types of fishing, depending on the type and location of the fish pursued. Fly rod development also included the employment of whalebone tips and, toward the end of the 1700s, the introduction of bamboo.

Anglers began blending their traditional horsehair lines with silk, which added much-needed line strength, eventually transitioning to full silk lines. This allowed for the formation of fly-line tapers and eliminated the need for troublesome knots at various locations of the line. This, in turn, aided in casting, the uptake of line on a reel, and other aspects of fly fishing. A terrific achievement: score one for the fly fisher. That left only one problem in this situation: silk is not especially buoyant. No one said this was easy.

A moment ago, I referred to the fishing reel. The use of longer fly lines was highly instrumental in the adoption of the fly reel as a standard piece of fly fishing hardware. Without one, long lines could easily get tangled at an angler's feet. The first fly reels, referred to variously as winches, winders, or multipliers, came about around 1650 and, frankly, were neither hardy nor sophisticated. But—they successfully stored the newly developed long silk fly lines and paved the way for more advanced reels.

In the latter half of the 1700s, the first Industrial Revolution begat mass production of fly lines, rods, and reels that became available in shops. This produced a sizeable increase in fly fishing participation. As railroads began to trace the transportation outlines of Northern Europe, anglers were better equipped to fish for other species such as salmon, and to share and trade knowledge more remotely.

Other innovations of this era, including tempered steel hooks and the introduction of fly fishing on lakes and ponds, made the sport accessible to more anglers. Heading into the 1800s, fly fishing innovation and participation continued to rise.

1800-1950

Fly fishing media, advertisements, and literature continued to flourish in the 1800s as fly fishing spread across Northern Europe. Alongside this boom came the debut of fishing magazines (circa the late 1800s). These new and growing media allowed innovations such as new fly patterns, knowledge of the fishing ecosystem, innovations in fly gear manufacturing, and, importantly, fish-based recipes to be shared, spread, and built upon, along with new fly fishing methods and gear.

Fishing clubs gained attendance, which spawned (no pun intended) a culture of fellowship. This gave anglers an additional opportunity to share information, observations, and brags, as well as giving them an outlet for their competitive spirits, a steady source of quality drinking spirits, and plenty of opportunities to build upon one of fishing's most celebrated traditions: The Great (Exaggerated) Fish Story.

Supported by many (but not all, to be fair) fishing clubs, this period also saw the introduction of catch-and-release fishing. Over the decades, catch-and-release has done wonders for this sport and the ecology and conservation of rivers, streams, and fish species.

During this period, we also saw the growth of fishing for recreation and enjoyment, rather than merely a means of sustenance. These concepts birthed the social divisions between fly fishing and spin/bait fishing still encountered today. Particularly in the early to mid-19th century, fly fishing was limited to landowners and those with enough money for leisure activities.

Fly fishing with nymphs significantly evolved during this time with the publication of the 1836 book *The Fly-Fisher's Entomology* by Alfred Ronalds. He is credited with being the first to identify specific fishing-centric insects and to standardize their names (for anglers). He also was a one-person bedrock institution, being among the very first persons to tie specific—i.e., insect—flies for fish species.

Speaking of flies, this is when dry flies took off as a preferred tool for anglers, changing forever the designation of some "people who fish" to "fly fishers."

Dedicated and specialized fly fishing shops, or fly shops, started popping up in the Catskills and other eastern U.S. hot spots in the 1920s. By the 1940s, a few shops had opened in western hot spots like West Yellowstone and Livingston, Montana.

Fly fishing also saw some diversification in the 1800s, with the introduction and rise of Spey fishing. Spey fishing, or Spey casting, involves using an 18- to 22-foot-long wooden two-handed rod, a different casting style (no overhead back cast), and large ornate flies for catching salmon. It was developed on the River Spey in Scotland and made catching salmon, once thought to be a fool's errand, easier.

Other advancements toward the middle to end of this period included standardized hook sizes, split cane bamboo rods, and the introduction of the first fiberglass rods.

Fly fishing had now arrived in the United States (no doubt at least in part due to mass European emigration) and had become a popular hobby. Vermont's Charles Orvis founded one of the most recognized names in the sport, The Orvis Company, in 1856. This firm still sells quality fly fishing gear and promotes the sport worldwide to this day. Orvis developed the first "modern" fly reel around this same time, along with many other contributions.

1950-Present

The current era of fly fishing has seen many minor modernizations and subtle advancements of established tackle and methods, but most of the already-existing tenets remain. Quality of materials; the durability of hardware and fishing lines alike; human-made lines in an avalanche of styles, colors, and purposes; advances in materials used to tie flies; and vast improvements in the comfort and waterproofing of fly fisher attire are among the most apparent advances of recent decades.

The inventory of fly fishing books and fly fishing magazines has waxed and waned over the years. The launch of the Internet has likely been responsible for promoting and advancing the sport in recent decades. Fly fishing blogs, photography, video, and social media have all become significant parts of the culture.

Guided fly fishing, which plodded along until 1992, gained a new lease on life when the movie *A River Runs through It* hit theaters. Robert Redford's adaptation of Norman Maclean's novella resonated strongly with the general public, and interest in fly fishing spiked—along with increased demand for guided fly fishing. That movie put fly fishing firmly on the map of American recreation.

Another fly fishing trend of this time is saltwater fly fishing. It had likely been going on for hundreds of years. Still, saltwater fly fishing's popularity as a sport truly skyrocketed in the 1950s, '60s, and '70s due to widespread financial stability amongst the angling class, along with anglers' natural propensity to explore new aquatic vistas.

Dynamic characters like Lefty Kreh, Ted Williams, and Lee Wulff heavily promoted saltwater and mangrove fly fishing. In the 1970s, the sport's most prominent writers, including Tom McGuane, Jim Harrison, and Richard Brautigan, took to calling Key West, Florida, home.

More recently, in the 1990s and 2000s, fly fishing for warm-water species like bass, panfish, pike, and musky has been well received, prompting the saying, "If it's a fish and it swims, it's fair game for fly angling these days."

Fish and fisheries conservation also exploded in the current era, with non-profits like Trout Unlimited and the Bonefish-Tarpon Trust attracting hundreds of thousands of enthusiastic followers. Movements like #KeepEmWet (which encourages anglers not to remove a fish from water longer than necessary to avoid killing fish that they intend to return to the water) achieved extensive influence. A robust ethical component of fish and fisheries stewardship has joined the sport.

Interestingly, while broad participation in fly fishing has remained steady over the past several years at about 2% of the total U.S. population, fly fishing participation among female U.S. anglers has exploded to about 25% of the fly fishing population over the last 15 or so years.

Early iterations of fly fishing like Spey and tenkara fishing are once again in vogue, as anglers look for different ways, both challenging and simplified, to approach fishing.

The sport of fly fishing has come a long way and will likely continue to be an essential part of outdoor water recreation for decades to come.

In Closing

As we have seen, fly fishing has evolved from a means of obtaining sustenance into a global multibillion-dollar land-and-sea sport. New materials have evolved the essential gear used by fly fishers. Yet the "basic gear" remains roughly the same: a fly rod, a fly reel, a fishing net, fly fishing line, and, of course, flies.

Also remaining the same are the basic tactics of understanding fly fishing's prey, how the fish use the river, how to read the rivers and streams, how to work the fly on the water, how to work a hooked fish, how to identify fly types for specific locations and times of the year, and of course, how to understand the fish themselves.

For this, we must be grateful. Now that you have a firm grounding in the history of this fantastic sport, let's head-on into the book.

Good luck, tight lines, and good fishing!

Introduction to the 1924 Edition

by Michael Temple (Edited)

I N THE STRICT SENSE of the term, nobody can teach anybody else to become a fly fisher. "Men (and women) are to be born so," and all the coaching and equipment in the world will do nothing for the pupil who does not have the right temperament.

Yet, when I ask myself in what that temperament consists, I find it very hard to find any genuinely satisfactory answer. If you are the pure fly fisher breed, you will have many days at the end of which you will come home with an empty creel and yet be able to say quite honestly that you have had an excellent day of sport fishing.

To the person who loves fly fishing, there is no sport in the world to which it compares.

To begin with, there is the unique attraction of pitting your wits against one of nature's most intriguing creations. One whose intelligence in its own line of business you will very soon come to have a very wholesome respect. If you occasionally win in that contest, the victory is something of which you can take pride. If occasionally (one hopes), you lose the battle, you can still admire—without resentment—the acuteness which foiled your utmost skill.

You are always fighting against difficulties: and their name is legion. Besides the sharp eyesight and cunning of the trout—both of which are almost uncanny—every new cast is a new problem. You may have encountered some of these:

- ✎ Here, it is a hawthorn behind you: a snag waiting to happen.
- ✎ There is a weed bed in the water in front of you.
- ✎ In another situation, you are aiming to cast your fly under a low-hanging branch.
- ✎ In a fourth situation, there is a stone or a bunch of loose rocks, which have obviously gotten where they are as an instance of malignant or malicious behavior of nature.

In the joy of fly fishing, there is no end to your troubles. However, it is just for that reason that the fascination inherent in the sport never fades. You may get tired of everything else, but, take my word for it, once a fly fisher, a fly fisher you will be to the end of your days.

Now despite what I've just written, fly fishing is no sport for a fool.

It demands, as few other sports do, the divine gift of imagination. If a person cannot enter the mind and the psychology of the fish, he had best go to the fish market to find the guest of honor at a family trout dinner. Because even the best fly assortment, most up-to-date equipment, and best expert training money can buy will have failed the dinner table.

Nor is fly fishing a sport for the person to whom the soul in Nature does not appeal.

Your true fly fisher loves the streams and all that go with them for their own sake. There is an exquisite delight in both the translucent depths framed in the lush river valleys and the brawling rapids of the mountain stream. Joy in the sounds of water and the tumble of even tiny cascades. Beauty in fields spangled with cowslip and native flowers and air laden with the scent of the water, earth, and the very air itself. Symphony in the blackbird, that unparalleled artist, as it pours forth a joyous soul in song, and the reed-warbler murmuring a tender song of love.

Should the fly fisher happen upon a natural rival in the entity of an otter or a heron, there is no anger in the fisher's heart. For are not nature's own also sisters and brothers of the hunt for a fish? To our angler, the small fish exactions of the kingfisher seem a paltry tax to pay for the enjoyment of watching, experiencing, that gem of living topaz and sapphire. And if the bird flits impudently over a rising trout, it is but waiting a minute for the fish to understand that the bird means it no harm.

Hearken to the words of Dame Juliana Berners, Prioress of Sopwell, in the first book on angling ever written in English:

"Atte the leest est he hath his holsom walke, and mery at his ease, a swete ayre of the swete savoure of the meede floures that makyth him hungry; he hereth the melodyous armony of fowles, he seeth the younge wannes: heerons: chickes: and many other foules with theyr brodes, whyche me semyth better than alle the noyse of houndys: the blastes of hornys, and the scrye of foulis that hunters, fawlkeners, and foulers can make. And if the angler take fysshe: surely henne is there noo man merier than he is in his spyryte."

If that be your "spyryte" (spirit), you are three parts fly fisher already. All a veteran angler may pretend to do is to give you the help of his or her experience in the art in the hope of making smooth your path to mastery and of saving you from some stumbles on the way.

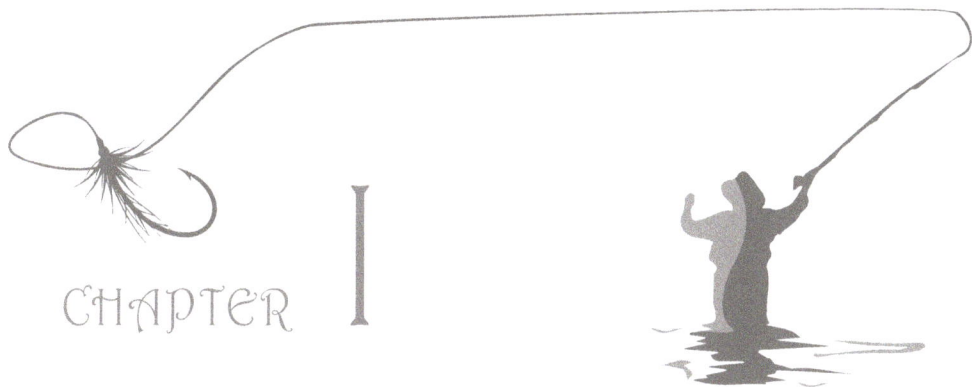

CHAPTER I

General Equipment

(1924 edition, edited)

THERE IS NO NEED to fit yourself out with all the newest and most expensive gadgets, and I am going to try to keep your expenditure on tackle as low as I can.

It is not necessary to have much, but what you have must be reliable and durable. It is often possible to pick up bargains at estate, garage, and yard sales. Failing that, shop a tackle maker with an established reputation and put yourself in their hands.

If you can persuade an experienced fly fisher friend to go with you when you go tackle shopping, so much the better.

But beware of cheap tackle. To *your* eye, any given piece of tackle may look no different from the work of a true craftsman—but it will most surely fail you in the hour of need.

Rods

Now, first as to the rod. One of the most intimidating choices for the new fly fisher is selecting the right fly rod for the fishing you wish to do.

I think it will be better for you to be content at first with a good, sound rod that is dependable and easy to mend on the spot when you've put your foot into a rabbit hole, and broken this-or-that aspect and expert assistance is fifty miles away.

Take care that the rod is not too heavy for you to use with comfort and that it feels light in hand. When the reel is on, it should have a balance at a point not more than a few inches above the grip, and the closer that point is to the grip, the more comfortable the rod will feel.

In terms of length, seven to ten feet is quite long enough. Another option: get a four- or five-weight rod. These are quite versatile and are suitable for a variety of targets from trout to bass. Fly rod manufacturers today sell the majority of their rods in 9-foot lengths.

The rod should err on the stiff than on the whippy side. I do not agree that a fly rod should be more rigid than any other. Those who say so are,

I fancy, only emphasizing their objection to excessive pliability of and in the rod. When you hold a ten-foot rod horizontally and the point drops from three to three and a half inches, it is just about right.

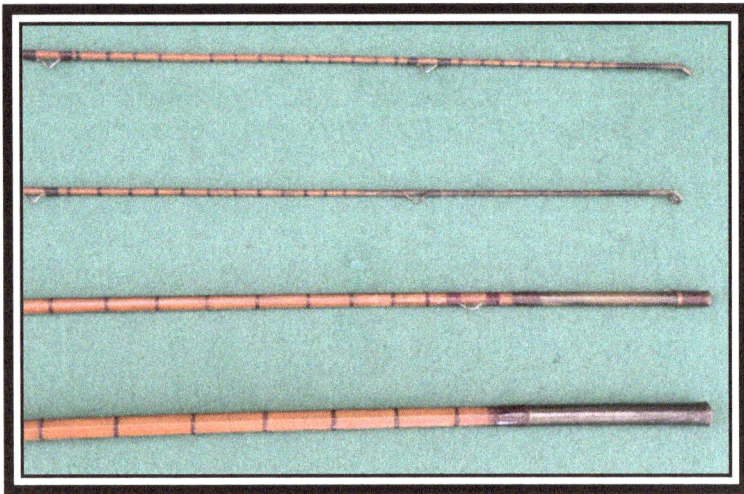

Figure 2 *Bamboo "Split Cane" Rod*

When in use, the rod should bend evenly from butt to point. There must be no "floppiness" about it anywhere along its length. And, if the rod is fitted with locked joints, so much the better.

Note that the foundation of any quality fly rod lies in the joints. Here is where the fly fisher depends on the balance and strength of the rod to withstand the power of large prey.

With such a rod, you can do anything of a fly fishing nature, within reason. And the odds favor your growing so fond of your rod that you will never discard it in favor of a more luxurious model. There is one such rod beside me as I write, which has been my friend and companion for forty years and has never failed me yet. It is as good today as when it left its maker's hands, and I would not change it for a wilderness of split-canes.

Reels

For most people who take their first steps in fly fishing, a fly reel may be thought of as merely something to hold the fly line and nothing more. Until the quality of the reel and its drag system are all that stands between the fly fisher and landing a 24-inch trout.

When you have years of on-the-river experience, you will appreciate the subtleties of more advanced fly reels. For now, let's agree to stay simple. Pick one that will comfortably hold the necessary amount of assembled fly line (more on this in the next chapter) for the weight of your rod.

For example, if you purchased a five-weight rod, buy a fly reel that will accommodate fly line weights from four to six. Most fly reels can handle a range of fly line weights. Ensure that you find yours within that range.

For the reel to hold your line and backing, there is nothing better than one made of gun-metal with two handles set flush in the face, so that there is nothing to catch the line at critical moments. Like rods, reels are made in different physical sizes as well.

The reel seat should be made of one solid piece of metal and be without any seams. It should be fastened to the rod butt in such a way as to prevent water from entering while also preventing the reel from coming loose.

The same can be said of the line guide: it should be unmarked and completely smooth and polished to allow for smooth line movement.

The reel should be large enough to hold at least thirty to fifty yards of line comfortably. Additionally, it should be fitted with an adjustable drag strong enough to prevent the line from over-running when you make a cast.

That one item—the drag system—is what keenly differentiates a $60 reel from a $400 reel. Don't overspend. But be diligent about checking user reviews and other media to ensure your reel and its drag system will hold up to the type (and size) of fish you will be pursuing.

Courtesy of *www.firstcastflyfishing.com,* here is a graphic showing the basic anatomy of a fly fishing reel.

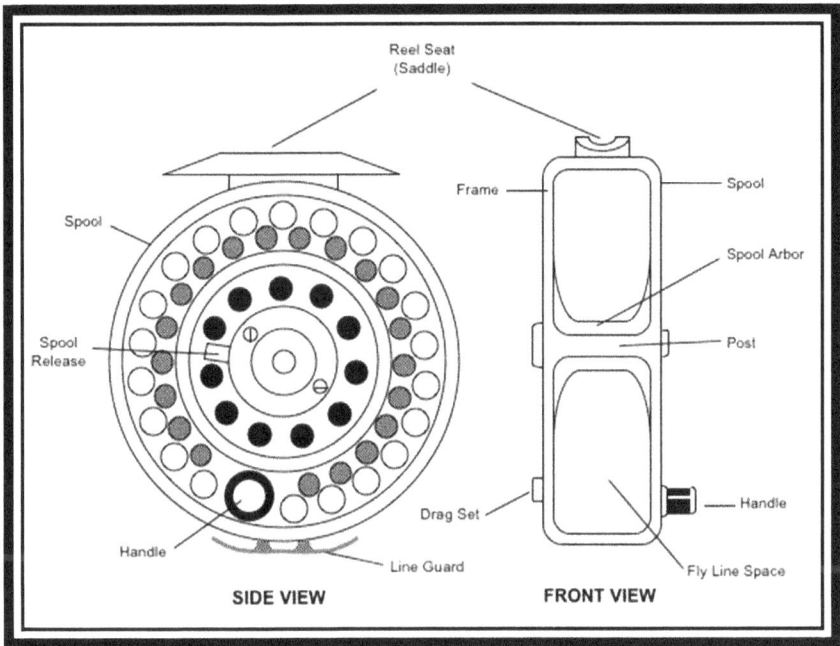

Figure 3 *Anatomy of a fly fishing reel.*
Photo courtsey www.firstcastflyfishing.com

There's
no
getting
away
from
'KINGFISHER'
LINES for trout
and salmon
OF ALL GOOD
TACKLE DEALERS

Line

Another critical issue in selecting a fly rod is establishing what line will be appropriate for your fishing plans. The size, as well as the fish species you plan to chase, will be the dominant factors in selecting the line weight for you.

Fly line comes in a variety of weights, indicated by a number from 1 to 14. Many authorities will recommend a particular line weight for a certain species of fish that will create the most "sporting" situation for the angler. Be careful here: often, these recommendations are a bit under-weighted and result in overplaying fish during a fight.

However, you need not to not only to consider the species of fish you're after when choosing a line weight but also the average weight of the flies you intend to cast. Experience tells: you can cast smaller flies with a heavier weight rod much more comfortably than you can cast heavier flies with a lighter weight rod

Lines are made of all sorts of materials and colors, but if you take my advice, you will have one matched to the weight of the rod. As to color choices, mine tend toward lighter colors as they are more readily visible on the water.

The weight of the line *must* be adjusted to the rod to be used. If it is too light for the particular rod, proper casting is almost impossible. If it is too heavy, it will strain the rod and wear it out in a surprisingly short time.

For this adjustment, I can give you very basic rule-of-thumb: "rod equals line." That is to say, if you have a five-weight rod, use as your default a five-weight fly line. It is the weight of the line that causes your fly rod to bend (with the weight/load of the line) when you cast.

Fly lines have a variety of attributes with which you must become familiar. For example, some fly lines float. Others are weighted to sink. My best advice here is to keep it simple during your first steps in fly fishing. It is quite possible to spend severe sums of money on lines, leaders, and supporting paraphernalia.

As to the length of the line you will need, here again, simple is best. In most cases, your fly casts will be less than 50 feet, often more like 20 feet. First-time fly fishers will most likely be casting within a 20-foot radius. So, while the overall line on your reel may be 150 to 200 feet due to leader construction, you'll probably only be working within a limited casting zone.

Another point is this: fly fishing line comes in different tapers, which define how the line is weighted. In general, there are three basic tapers: weight forward (this is the most commonly used taper), double taper, and level taper. Here is wisdom: in your first steps in fly fishing, procure a moderate weight forward taper. It's an excellent middle-of-the-road selection.

That seems like quite a bit of information, and so it is.

Here may I suggest another simple path. A short conversation with the fly fishing expert who sells you your rod and reel will no doubt yield you a proper line for your first activities. And, at a price you can afford. So, if you will forgive a turn of phrase, let us not get hung up on the intricacies of lines. Let us instead turn our attention to how a proper trout leader is assembled.

Wait—one other essential item regarding lines: at the end of the day, proper cleaning of your line is always "money in the bank." Forward.

A trout leader is generally arranged into three primary sections. I will let Tony Pearse of *Fishswami.com*[1] explain how the different sections are used and constructed into a proper trout leader:

Leader Construction

Leaders are constructed of 3 sections: the butt, taper, and tippet. The butt section should be made from stiff monofilament to transfer energy well. The butt section is 60% of the total length. The tippet is the section that presents the fly to the fish. It should be supple for a good presentation. The taper is the section between the butt and the tippet, and it should be short.

Whenever possible, do not connect monofilament line pieces differing in diameter of more than 2/100ths of an inch (.02"). They will not transfer energy well, and the knots are not as strong.

Also, larger differences can cause a hinging effect when you cast. The diameter of the butt section of the leader should match the fly line weight (the butt section should be about 2/3rds the diameter of the fly line).

Most leaders you buy in the store only match a 5 or 6 weight (wt) line. They don't work well on a lighter line *or* a heavier line. A 3wt line should have a butt section of .018-.020; a 4wt .019-.021; a 5wt .020-.022; a 6wt .021-.023; a 7wt .022-.024; an 8wt. .023-.026 and a 9 wt .024-.027.

---

1 With our profound thanks to Mr. Pearse's article "Hand Tying Fly Leaders," 3/24/2008, www.fishswami.com.

The blood or barrel knot is typically used for the butt and taper sections. It takes some practice to tie well, but it is good because the line comes out evenly on each side of the knot. One tip for tying the blood knot is to use 3 wraps with heavier mono in the butt section and 4-5 wraps in the taper.

The double surgeon's knot is used for the tippet sections as it has greater strength. If you are tying two different brands of materials together (including fluorocarbon), use a triple surgeon's knot for extra slip protection.

Always wet the knots before drawing them tight to ensure the knots are tight and don't heat up and weaken as they are tightened. This is especially important for fluorocarbon! Pull the knots very tight (you may want to wear work-gloves) and then trim the knots close. If you are concerned about the knots catching moss, you can put a thin coat of Loon KnotSense over them to help smooth them out.

Leader to Fly Line Connection

There are 2 popular options for attaching the leader to the fly line. The first is to connect a section of butt material to the fly line using a nail knot. Then whenever a new leader is needed, you attach it to the butt material using a blood knot. This way, you don't have to keep cutting pieces of fly line, and you don't have to tie a nail knot out on the river!

The second option is to use a loop-to-loop connection. Some fly lines have a loop on them. You can also tie a loop in the end of the piece of butt section that is attached to the fly line. Keep the loops small and use a perfection loop as it ties in a straight line (keep the loops small, so they go through the guides smoothly).

"A picture is worth a thousand words," so with thanks to *www.fishswami.com*, let us finally look at the typical construction of a trout leader.

Perfection
Loop

Blood
Knot

Blood
Knot

Butt
Section

Maxima
Clear
36"
.022"

Maxima
Clear
16"
.020"

Maxima
Clear
12"
.017"

Blood
Knot

Surgeon's
Knot (3)

Blood
Knot

Taper
Section

Rio
Powerflex
6"
.010" 1X

Maxima
Clear
6"
.012"

Maxima
Clear
6"
.015"

Surgeon's
Knot (2)

Surgeon's
Knot (2)

Tippet
Section

Rio
Powerflex
12"
.008" 3X

Rio
Powerflex
24"
.007" 4X

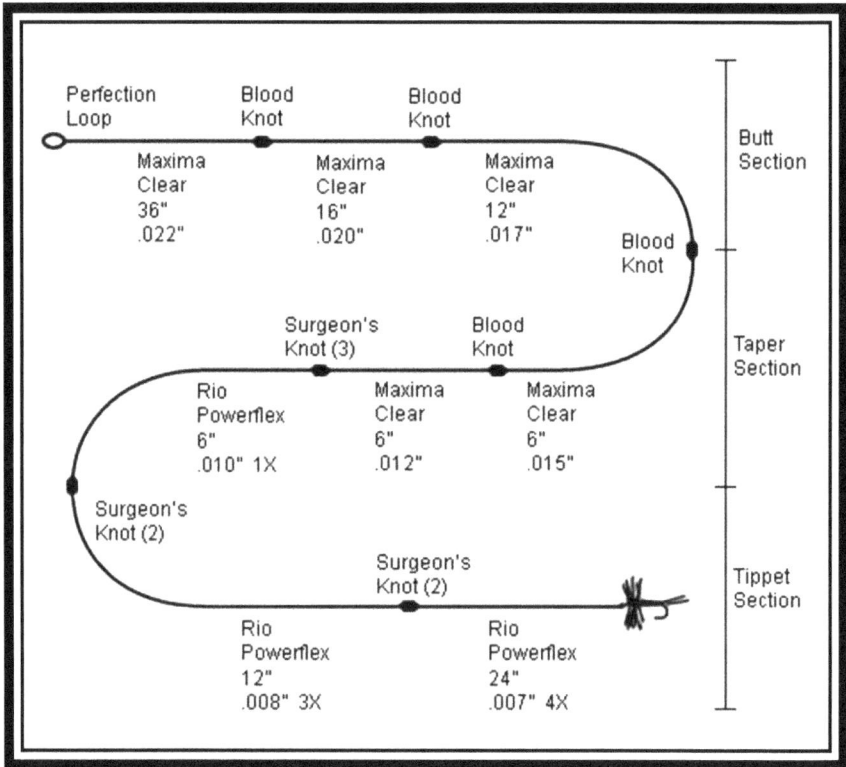

Figure 4 *Sections of a trout leader.*
Photo generously supplied by www.fishswami.com.

Again, in closing, let me reiterate: If you're just taking your first steps in fly fishing, keep it simple. Just buy a floating weight forward line that matches the weight of your rod, learn the perfection loop, and master the blood knot and the surgeon's knot—and onward!

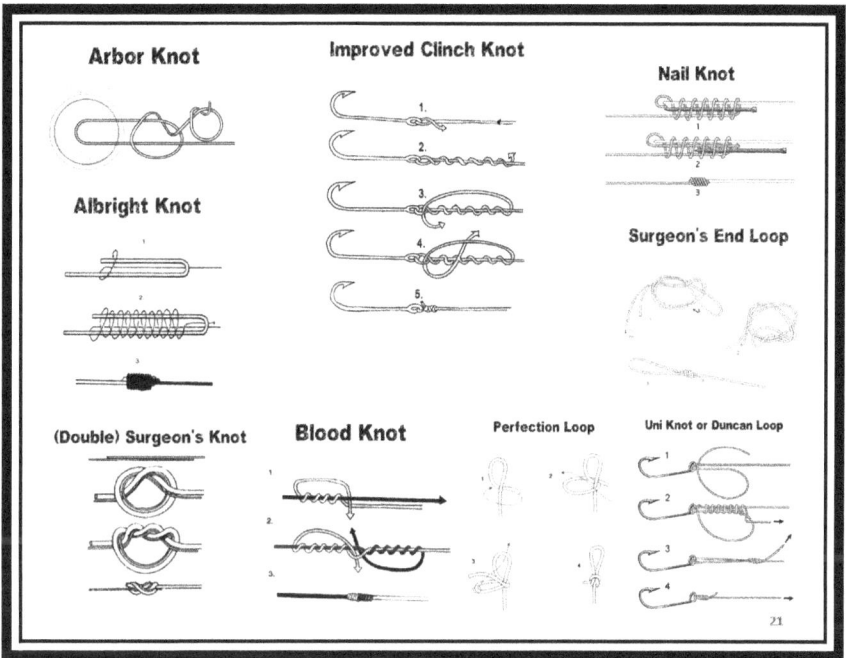

Figure 5 *Basic fly fishing knots and loops.*

MINNOW BUCKETS

MAGIC

Round, non-floating IC tin bucket. No cover. Inset made of perforated tin, with hinged perforated, self-locking cover. Finished in blue japan and gold striping. Large wire bail with wood grip.

NOS. 100 AND 80

No.	Capacity	Size	Wt. each	Each
100	10 qts.	9½x9¼ in.	3½ lbs.	$2.00
80	8 qts.	8¾x8¾ in.	3 lbs.	1.70

SPLENDID

Round, single IC tin bucket. Wired top. Sunk, perforated cover with hasp and staple. Finished in green japan and gold striping. Large wire bail with wood grip.

No. 8

No.	Capacity	Size	Wt. each	Each
8	8 qts.	8¾x8¾ in.	1½ lbs.	$1.30

All the above, loose.

MINNOW TRAP

Gee's improved minnow trap is made of heavy grade, galvanized wire cloth and is wired at each end. Ends or halves are exactly alike, thereby doing away with mistakes in shipping. Each trap is furnished with a snap, one end to hold trap together and the other suitable to tie a rope or cord into.

	Size	Wt. each	Each
Minnow Trap	17½x9 in.	2¼ lbs.	$1.70

Six in a crate.

FISH BASKETS

SPLIT WILLOW

NOS. 0-S TO 6-S

Bleach willow, woven very tight. Hole to one side. Patent cover fasteners.

No.	Capacity	Base measurement	Wt. each	Each
0-S	6 lbs.	10 in.	⅝ lb.	$2.30
1-S	9 lbs.	12 in.	¾ lb.	2.80
2-S	12 lbs.	13 in.	1 lb.	3.20
3-S	20 lbs.	14 in.	1¼ lbs.	3.50
4-S	25 lbs.	15 in.	1½ lbs.	4.00
5-S	30 lbs.	16 in.	2 lbs.	4.50
6-S	35 lbs.	17 in.	2¼ lbs.	5.00

WHOLE WILLOW

(Plain cover fasteners.)

No.	Capacity	Base measurement	Wt. each	Each
0-W	6 lbs.	10 in.	⅝ lb.	$1.40
1-W	9 lbs.	12 in.	¾ lb.	1.60
2-W	12 lbs.	13 in.	1 lb.	1.80
3-W	20 lbs.	14 in.	1¼ lbs.	2.20
4-W	25 lbs.	15 in.	1½ lbs.	2.40

SPLIT WILLOW, LEATHER BOUND

NOS. 2-L TO 6-L

Bound with genuine horsehide, hand sewed. Leather handle, buckle and strap fastener.

No.	Capacity	Base measurement	Wt. each	Each
2-L	12 lbs.	13 in.	1¼ lbs.	$ 6.00
3-L	20 lbs.	14 in.	1½ lbs.	7.00
4-L	25 lbs.	15 in.	1¾ lbs.	8.20
5-L	30 lbs.	16 in.	2 lbs.	8.70
6-L	35 lbs.	17 in.	2¼ lbs.	10.00

Note—Prices on fish baskets do not include basket straps.

All the above, loose.

Other Equipment

You will need something in which to carry your fish and your tackle, and nothing is better than the ordinary basket-weave creel. Avoid all bags, haversacks, and waterproof abominations. They spoil the appearance of your hard-won trout, and it is an everlasting problem to keep them clean.

For your creel, put some hay in the bottom of your basket to prevent the contents from jostling. It will keep sweet and clean for years.

Next, a landing-net is also an indispensable addition to your equipment. A 12-inch landing net is sufficient for most pond and stream fishing.

Also, put a "priest," commonly known as a poacher's, warden's, or angler's priest, or as a "fish bat," in your kit for the administration of last rites to your fishing prize. This sort of priest is a small club with a bit of metal weight at the top. A tap with it just behind the head will kill your fish instantly. Always carry one with you because it is barbarous to leave the unhappy trout to expire in prolonged agonies of suffocation. Secondly, because if you leave the fish to drown in the air or kill them in any other way, they are apt to die with their mouths open and present a gruesome spectacle.

I am afraid that you must have waders. As to the sort, you may suit yourself and your purse: all that really matters is that they should keep out water. But some kind of waders are a necessity, for without them you cannot, on many streams, get properly and inconspicuously to your fish at all.

If you elect to use waterproof fishing-stockings with a pair of brogues to be worn over them, put very coarsely knitted socks between your stockings and shoes. Otherwise, intrusive gravel will speedily wear holes in the waterproofing, and the tiniest puncture will be quite enough to give you the most effective soaking.

When wading, go slowly and disturb the water as little as you can. Fish are intensely sensitive to vibrations in the water and disturbances on the surface. The fly fisher who goes walloping about in a still section of a stream or river, sending waves in front of himself or herself, will infallibly put down every rising fish.

If, by accident, you make a disturbance of any kind, keep quiet until it has subsided. The trout will conclude that the bother was caused by some clumsy but harmless cow or sheep and begin to feed again.

As to whether you should have a fly book or a fly box? Well, please yourself.

Fly boxes are in fashion now, but I still prefer a leather fly book with plenty of pockets for spare leaders and the like. It should also have places for a small pair of scissors (mine are Hardy "Bent Blade" scissors), nippers, and a small disgorging tool.

My fly book is of alternate leaves of felt and parchment. In the felt, I stick the flies, and on the (parchment) paper, I write any notes referring to the flies that seem worth remembering.

People say that it spoils the "set" of the flies to keep them in this way, but I have never found it so myself, and the book allows you to have everything to your hand at once, which a box does not. I keep one felt page at the end for flies that I wish to put away damp. The felt dries them well enough, and they do not injure the others in the process.

Whether you prefer a book or a box, take every precaution to keep moths away. There is nothing more maddening than to find that the moths have gotten at your flies when your back was turned, and the brutes always seem to choose one's special flies for their depredations.

While we are on the subject of precautions, let me return, briefly, to the question of line. How long yours will last is directly related to four items: grime or dirt, sunlight, storage, and usage. Mind these "four horsemen" and your line and leaders will last for many a trip. Neglect even one, and you will see the difference in unresponsive or break-prone line. Clean, dry, and dark are your watchwords here.

Similarly, I keep a Hardy "Drianoil" Fly Oiler in my pocket as well. It is a pocket watch case, modified to hold a felt pad for oiling flies, and an amadou pad (a spongy material derived from a natural tree fungus (Fomes formentarius)) for drying flies. There are other similar devices on the market, but none are a patch to a genuine Hardy. Their Waistcoat Pocket Fly Oil Bottle is always in my kit, too.

Hardy produces a reel oiler, as well. Quite a handy little tool that fits easily in one's pocket to address a balky reel. Last but not least, in my pantheon of "All Things Hardy" is their "Wardle." It's a small magnifying glass that pins to one's jacket, and that conveniently folds out of the way when not in use. Brilliant!

Moving along, Farlow Company manufactures a "Net Ring." It gives fly fishers a means of keeping their fishing net (see above) at hand. The Net Ring also attaches to one's fishing jacket with a stout pin. To use, one simply slides the handle of the net through the ring, and your fishing net is secure, but immediately at hand. Ingenious.

⁎⁎⁎

You will think I am never going to be done with my gadgets and suggestions, but if you will suffer me to recommend just one more, I promise you it shall be the last.

There is a most useful little arrangement consisting of a rather heavy metal ring that can be opened to place it around your rod. To this is attached a length of fine but strong cord. The object of the whole contraption is to save you from a bad break when you get into difficulties—as you certainly will.

Suppose you get your fly fixed in a sturdy hawthorn. When you do, it generally happens that, owing to the depth of the water, or the height of the banks, or something or other, there is no getting at the blessed thing. Here the clearing-ring will save you.

Slip it on the rod and let it slide down the line until it reaches the point at which you are stuck. Then pull on the cord. If you are lucky, you will bring the detainer away: if you are not, you will at least lose no more than the fly instead of half your leader as well.

It is a simple little contrivance, costing truly little, and taking up hardly any room. It is also most efficient and will save you many a breakage. Besides, the mere knowledge that you have it in your pocket will give you confidence in casting into the near neighborhood of danger.

CHAPTER II

Flies

(1924 edition, edited & 21st Century)

W E COME NOW TO the flies themselves, the imitations by which we hope to deceive the fish. Their name, their very look, are legion. Unfortunately, you need to be careful: sometimes, a variety may have several names of its own according to the locality, or who or what is merchandising the fly in question.

The entomology of fly fishing is an intricate if attractive science. I hope to be able to simplify it for you to a considerable extent. Still, you are not to suppose that you can safely dispense with all knowledge of the subject. As we shall see, the fly is meant to represent the fish's preferred food, and you need to be aware.

Speaking of fly fishing, back in what I may perhaps venture to call the Fly Fisher Dark Ages, people tried an odd assortment of methods to attract their quarry. One of the most bizarre had to be this: a cast *of a dozen flies on the same leader* was quite commonly employed! And an extraordinarily clumsy thing it must have been.

Then, as the trout grew warier and more thoughtful fishing became necessary, the number of flies flung at the poor fish was reduced to two or three at once on a single leader. And to that, a surprising number of those who fly fish still adhere to this day.

Fortunately for those taking their first steps in fly fishing today, one might say that common sense prevails. Today the use of a single fly only, even when one is fishing "wet," that is, allowing the fly to sink below the surface, is the norm.

I am so convinced that this is the best approach that I am not going to trouble you with any directions for other methods. Yes, over time, collect a variety of flies. But when fishing, find the fly that is the right one for the time, the location, and conditions and start with that one (singular) fly. In essence, it is that simple.

Let us move on to selecting the fly itself.

On streams or lakes whose trout are very little fished for, almost any fly will do well enough at times. That is, I think because a great many of them bear a general resemblance to natural insects. Others tempt fish by their very strangeness and are taken for the same mysterious reason(s) that induces a salmon to rise at creations which are like nothing found in any of the waters of the earth.

But I have never found the local "fail-me-never" a whit better, even on such unfished waters as are now rare, than an imitation of the fly that is, or lately has been, on the water.

While on streams whose trout are educated and often subject to severe fishing pressure, fly selection can become even more of an art than a science. And yet, while speaking of science, one can cautiously agree that it may be tiresome to study the entomology of the water. It stands to reason that if the trout takes an artificial fly by mistaking it for the natural insect, the closer you can get to Nature in selecting and deploying such a fly, the more successful you will be.

As I mentioned a moment ago, the entomology of fly-fishing is a science in itself. It is more than likely that in your progress from Entered Apprentice to Master Fish Craftsperson, you will become fascinated by it.

Fortunately, however, it is not at all necessary to acquire any profound knowledge of the subject at the outset or to lay in a stock of flies that resemble all of the multitudinous varieties of insect which appear from time to time on the water.

What science imports you to know and to have is a much simpler thing than that. There are specific varieties of insects which, because of their abundance, are always in the recollection of the fish. These you must have. You must learn over time to be able to recognize the natural insects when you see them on the water. You must also know the time of year at which their appearance is to be expected. Be patient. Gathering this knowledge comes with experience.

With a comparatively small stock of flies, you may not, perhaps, have an imitation of the insect at which the fish are rising at the moment.

Never mind. Out of one of the two lists I propose to give you, you will undoubtedly be able to pick one at which they were rising an hour or two ago and will be rising again an hour or two hence.

To be sure, there *are* indeed times when they will not look at anything except the one fly which is on for the moment. Well, if that is so, you cannot help it. But as a general rule, they will not disregard those whose flavor they have learned to appreciate, and whose appearance at the moment in question does not strike them as suspicious.

In support of Mr. Thoreau, to simplify the fly selection matter as much as possible, I will only give lists of the flies that consensus has voiced as indispensable.

But please understand that these really are indispensable.

They will all be useful, more or less, at their respective seasons, whether they are on the water or not, and, when they are on, the fish, in nine cases out of ten, will take nothing else.

Let me, however, add a cautionary note to my list.

Certain waters have their own peculiarities in the matter of flies. Here and there, you will come across a stream that specializes in the production of some insect, which is not included here. Only local knowledge can help you in these cases, which, happily, are not quite common, and such knowledge is easily acquired through the locals who fish this passage.

A last item, please.

We have decided to leave the original 1924 series of flies in first order followed by the 21st Century series. This not only serves the continuity of the original 1924 text, but it also demonstrates how the look of dry flies have changed over the years, and how the orthodoxy for how to fish them has also morphed.

With that, let us to the lists.

The 1924 Collection: Classics Then, Still Reliable Now

(1924 edition, edited)

The 1924 Collection: I—The Blue Dun

There are only two objections I know of regarding this capital fly. The first one is that it varies a good deal in shade, owing chiefly I think to differences of water/air temperatures when it hatches. As such, the wise fly fisher should carry at least two dressings, one light and one of a darker tint approaching almost to an olive-brown. The second reason is that in a sport that takes fly names *very* seriously, this particular fly sets the pace: it rejoices in a most confusing multiplicity of names.

As just one regional example, in many places in England, this fly is called the Hare's Ear. In Devonshire, England, the Blue Upright. Over in Yorkshire, it's called the Water-hen Bloa. And in North Lancashire and Cumberland, folks refer to the Blue Bloa or the Olive Bloa, according to the shade.

In fact, there is no end to the local names for this all-around favorite regardless of country or even region. But that need not trouble you, because any tackle-maker will know well enough what you mean when you say, "I require a Blue Dun, please?"

The fly makes its appearance in March. When the spring weather is pleasant, the lighter-coated version of this fly—which is the more usual

variety—will be most abundant. Conversely, when the weather is bleak, you'll do better with the darker form. In either form, use the Blue Dun until the end of May or so. That said, keep an eye out, as natural hatches occur from time to time throughout the season.

Figure 6 *The Blue Dun, Sample 1*
Photo courtsey FlyShack.Com

Figure 7 *The Blue Dun, Sample 2*
Photo courtsey FlyShack.Com

The 1924 Collection: II—The March Brown

Taking it all round, there is no better fly than this.

Except in a very genial season, it will rarely, despite its name, be found on the water before the beginning of April. But once it is on, it is a case of *J'y suis, j'y reste*, for it lasts until the coming of the mayfly.

In the late summer, it produces another hatch which, willfully enough, is called the August Dun, but is then somewhat smaller, so you will do well to have the fly in two sizes.

Its metamorphosis is the Red Spinner, which is abundant enough when the March Browns begin to shed their skins after the first stage in their winged life is over. I *do not* consider it indispensable.

Trout much prefer the March Brown and see nothing odd in the appearance among a lot of Red Spinners of a March Brown who has not yet changed his coat.

Let me add that if you cannot catch fish with the March Brown when the March Brown is "up," there is no fly that will ever be any good to you at all.

The March Brown also comes in some robust variants, including, in no particular order, the:

- Brindle Chute
- Carnage Western March Brown
- Epoxy Back Rubberleg Pheasant Tail Nymph
- Parachute Hare's Ear
- Parachute Pheasant Tail
- Umpqua Pheasant Tail Tungsten Jig

Figure 8 *The March Brown, American variant*
Photo courtsey The Fly Shack

"Fly fishing... requires an intimacy with bugs, birds, weather, water, and fish that sticking a worm on a hook never asked of me."

~ Ailm Travler ~

The 1924 Collection: III—The Yellow Dun

This fly, which in the north has the name of the Yellow-legged Bloa, is, I fancy, another variety of the Blue Dun.

But it is so different in color as to be, from the fisherman's point of view, entirely separate. In most waters, you will not find it until April is well advanced. But after the first arrival, when it is very abundant, it makes sporadic appearances throughout the season and is almost always much favored by the trout.

As to where to fish this or any other dun, let me state that there is a simple, preferred way to select your location. Rivers sometimes follow a three-step pattern, that of the riffle, the run, and the pool. When the water grade increases the volume and velocity of water, the water, in turn, will pile up rocks and other debris into the riffles. After the riffle, a run will concentrate the water. So it is that the run portion of this water pattern is where you should fish dry fly duns.

It is *always* well to keep one's eyes open for a rise of the Yellow Dun.

Finally, according to no less an authority than *www.guiderecommended. com*[2], these dun flies are also quite useful:

- **Mahogany Dun**, a common mayfly that has prolific hatches in the spring. A go-to fly for many pieces of water. The size 12 and red/brown color are an excellent fly for matching many hatches.

- **Comparadun**, marked by the upright wings bending toward the head. A great fly in size 12 to 16. Usually, the wings are a lighter color, making these flies easy to see.

- **Sulfur;** usually, the bright yellow is a dead giveaway for this fly. Look for hatches in the spring—May, and sometimes even early June. Watch for these pretties in the morning.

- **Blue Wing Olive**, a favorite wintertime fly when the sun pops out in the afternoon. Size 14 to 18 is good; look for those sunny patches of water from September to April.

---

2 *Copy courtesy of www.guiderecommended.com. Thank you!*

Figure 9 *The Sulpher Yellow Dun*
Photo courtsey of The Fly Crate

"Never forget:
Fly fishing is fun partly
because it is frustrating."

~ Phil Monahan ~

The 1924 Collection: IV—The Black Spider

Whether this fly is an imitation of any specific insect, and if so of which, I am not sure. I fancy its value lies in its resemblance to many small black flies, including that horrid little nuisance, the Black Gnat, some of which are almost always on the water.

But, whatever the explanation, there is no doubt about its usefulness, especially in clear water, and when there is no marked rise of anything else. Fished in the 12 to 24 inches of the water column, it's a terrific fly during a buzzer hatch on lake or river.

To be truly effective, fish spiders upstream, in much the same way as you would a nymph. Select what appears to be a likely fish holding location and cast to it, raising your rod tip as the flies drift back toward you. Stay on your toes, as this is a quick fishing method based on short drifts.

Also of note, the Black Spider fly is essential for all rough stream fishing anywhere in the world.

The best pattern is one that I believe should be dressed down "hackle-wise"; that is, without wings, with the feather of a cock-starling, and a body of brown silk. Size 26-30 Black Spider flies are quite popular, and you can hardly have it too small in size.

Our fellow fly fishers at *www.barbless-flies.co.uk*[3] have a splendid model called the "Across and Down" for fishing this fly:

"ACROSS AND DOWN"

The most common way to start fishing a team of spiders is to employ the "Across and Down" approach. Here are a few tips:

- Start at the head of the pool/riffle you want to fish
- Cast at 45 degrees across the flow
- Let the river flow move your flies downstream and then let them swing across the flow
- Keep your rod at 45 degrees to the water, so there is a slight sag in the line (allows better take detection)
- At the end of the swing across the current, wait a few seconds and then pull a couple of feet back in. This often induces a take, so be ready!

---

3 *Copy courtesy of* www.barbless-flies.co.uk. *Thank you!*

- Step down the river and repeat the above steps

The Across and Down method is great for searching water and is also a great way to start Spider fishing.

Figure 10 *Black Spider Fly*
Photo courtsey Peaks Fly Fishing

The 1924 Collection: V—The Iron Blue Dun

This fly, which is identical to the Little Dark Watchet of the north, generally makes its first appearance during some sudden gleam of sunshine as April merges into May.

It has a short season, but the fish have a great fancy for it while it lasts, and it is almost hopeless to try anything else when the Iron Blue is "up."

You may not want the Iron Blue for more than a week in the season, but when you do want it, you want it very badly indeed. You may expect a rise of it at any time from the end of April to the beginning of June.

Here's what J. Edson Leonard had to say about the Iron Blue Dun in 1950:

> There are perhaps as many variations of the Iron Blue as there are iron blues in your favorite stream.
>
> Fly-makers make this fly in shades from light brown to near black. Few imitations even remotely resemble the natural insect.
>
> The Iron Blue is as necessary to the fly-box as tobacco is to your pipe; therefore, its colors should be known.

Returning to our friends at *www.guiderecommended.com*[4], they suggest the following five tips for fly fishing a dun:

5 Tips for Fly Fishing a Dun"

"Often during a large hatch, your fly is just another of the thousands floating by a hungry trout. When this happens, change things up a little. For example, bump up the size of the fly you're using or even cut back the hackle to cripple the fly.

Timing and observation; I'll bet you eat dinner on a schedule. Trout do the same thing, so watch a rising fish and count off the rhythm in your head.

If you're floating in a boat and see a rise rising ahead, stop and give yourself time to make the right cast to the rising fish.

The big switch; if you've tied on 7 flies with no results, switch things up big. I've often switched to a Dry-Dropper setup at these times.

---

4   *Copy courtesy* www.guiderecommended.com, *with our thanks!*

Duns will float in water lanes close to the bank. You might lose some flies getting caught in the streamside brush, cast into those areas. When the right cast + a good drift + fishy water come together, it's truly like magic watching a trout rise.

Solid advice. Finally, be aware that this fly may also be found traveling by such names as the Blue Quill or Slate Drake. Some say there are as many as twenty different names for this versatile fly.

Figure 11 *Iron Blue Dun, Sample 1*
Photo courtesy The Essential Fly

Figure 12 *Iron Blue Dun, Sample 2*
Photo courtsey Dragonflies.co.uk

The 1924 Collection: VI—The Alder

Some fly fishers and fly fishing books suggest this particular fly may have been developed around 1496 when it was included in Dame Juliana Berners's first fly fishing book, *Fysshe and Fysshynge*.

According to Larry Bordas[5], writing on *www.flyanglersonline.com*:

> The Alder is a very old fly that has been tied in England for hundreds of years.
>
> Most of the Alder patterns we see today are reflective of those early English flies. (Some say) the lack of success with copies of the English flies might be explained because the English insect has a slightly different color than the American alder.
>
> (Some writers) take it one step farther and even separate the American Alder found in the East from the Western version and offer flies to match. Other authors and tiers have noticed this difference and have made small adjustments to copy the insect found on this side of the Pond.
>
> In his book *Flies*, J. Edson Leonard lists eight different versions of the alder.

In any event, it is undoubtedly a well-established fly and known to generations of fly fishers.

From the middle of May to the end of June, the Alder is abundant in most streams. This fly is of great use, especially toward evening, on days when the mayfly does not compete with it.

Being a decidedly stout insect, the imitation should be dressed with a much fuller body than is desirable in the case of the more delicate duns and spinners.

Alder flies can be fished dry, or by using an Alder wet fly as a sunk Alder, or as an Alder Larva Nymph.

Alderflies are close relatives of dobsonflies, and their larvae resemble the better-known hellgrammites. The Alder has the advantage of being an easy fly to imitate, and the trout are extraordinarily fond of it.

---

5   Copy courtesy *www.flyanglersonline.com*, *with our thanks!*

Figure 13 *Alder Wet Fly*
Photo courtsey dragonflies.co.uk

*"A fly fisher's knowledge is
compounded of many things.
It grows out of imagination,
curiosity, bold experiment, and
intense observation."*

~ Roderick Haig-Brown ~

The 1924 Collection: VII—The Dotterel

The Dotterel is very famous, being good not only of itself but as a passable imitation of many small flies that come on from time to time. Its namesake is the feather of the Dotterel bird.

You cannot do without it, for when the fish are rising at this fly, it is tough to persuade them to attend to anything else.

This and the Alder will be your standard flies for the interval—roughly the month of May—between the March Brown and the Mayfly. The Dotterel can also be quite effective on rather cold days.

Figure 14 *The Dotterel or "Little Blue"*
Courtesy of www.orvis.com

The 1924 Collection: VIII—
The Green Drake Mayfly / Gray Drake Mayfly

Mayfly varieties such as the Green Drake and the Gray Drake are, without a doubt, members of one of the most elegant of the insect species in the field of fly fishing.

In addition to being one of the trout's most important foods, they also trace an ancient lineage dating back to prehistoric times!

According to Břetislav Kašpar[6] on *www.globalflyfisher.com*:

> The first known appearance of the term "drake" was in Dame Juliana Berners's (1496) *"Treatyse of Fysshynge with an Angle."* The book uses the term "drakes" to describe fly patterns constructed by using feathers from a male duck.
>
> The next recorded tribute to the green drake comes from Charles Cotton, in the fifth edition (1676) of Walton's *"The Compleat Angler"* - "... of all these (and I have named you a great many very killing flies) none are fit to be compared with a Drake and Stone-fly, both for many and very great fish ..."

The majority (but by no means all) of mayfly species molt in the spring and early summer. However, I've been told of hatches in early spring and as late as mid-fall. So keep an eye on the water to see if these beauties are still at work. These in-between or off-season hatches could prove most rewarding for the fly fisher!

In most waters, the great rise of this fly is during the first two weeks in June. This provides what is rather unkindly known as "The Duffer's Fortnight," for the trout are greedy after it beyond all belief.

The Green Drake, *generally speaking*, is an emerger (mayflies in the molting phase are called emergers) and/or dun stage of a mayfly species. These are commonly green or pale olive.

Because of specific functions of a protein when combined (or not combined) with oxygen, the Green Drake is also known as the Gray Drake. When the protein is not oxygenated, it turns gray, and thus Green becomes Gray.

This must be made clear: the colors of Drakes vary a lot in different waters. This cannot be overstated. And a cunning old trout of years and discretion has a most acutely developed color sense.

---

6 *Copy courtesy Břetislav Kašpar on www.globalflyfisher.com, with our thanks!*

Fishing with Green Drakes can be exciting and tough—especially when so many real insects are on the same water. Moreover, these flies are certainly large enough to be carefully inspected by a wary trout—and refused!

All that said—should some kind, gentle fisher person tell you the green drakes are hatching, drop everything, grab a fly rod, and run to the water! You may just have one of the most productive days of fly fishing in the year.

Figure 15 *Mayfly Dun.*
Photo courtesy Orvis Corp

Figure 16 *Gray Drake Mayfly.*
Photo courtesy Alaska Fly Fishing Goods

The 1924 Collection: IX—The Coch-Y-Bonddu (also spelled Bondhu)

The Coch-y-Bonddu originated sometime in the 1700s. Back then, it was known as the Shorn Fly. One of the first things one learns about this fly is that it has a bewildering list of names. These include, in addition to Coch-Y-Bonddu, June Bug, Field Chafer Coch-y-Bondhy, Welshman's Button, Hazel Fly, Fern Web, Bracken Clock, and Marlow Buzz, among the rest.

In any event and as a general rule of thumb, they all refer to a little rotund beetle (Latin name, *Phylopertha horticola*).

It is a useful pattern in sizes 6-14 and effective as early as mid-May if trout start feeding on beetles. This fly imitates both aquatic beetles and terrestrial species that have fallen into a stream. While the Coch-y-Bonddu may indeed resemble an aquatic or drowned beetle, it also bears a striking resemblance to a variety of other subsurface insects.

It is not a stretch to say that this fly's inherent "bug look," combined with its long history of success at end-of-day, makes it a genuinely all-purpose utility fly.

It is typically seen, as one of its names implies, in largest concentrations in June. Notwithstanding that date limit, this is a really capital fly all through the season after the mayfly has disappeared and can be successful all season.

Suffice it to say; it is a must for wild trout.

Figure 17 *Coch y Bonddu*
Photo courtesy www.theessentialfly.com

The 1924 Collection: X and XI— The Red and Black Ants

In July, the winged ants come in thousands on to the water and are greedily taken by the fish.

During the dog days of summer, hundreds, even thousands, of ants fall from vegetation along the banks of the water. Moreover, flying ants simply nosedive on to the water's surface to the glee of waiting trout.

Generally speaking, you do not get both on the same stream, so, if you can discover which of the two affects the stream you fish, you can do without the other. Ants are also found in many lakes, too.

Otherwise, you must be prepared for either. The July hatches are slightly lighter in color than those of the spring.

The Ant is a must in any serious fly fisher's fly box.

Figure 18 *Black Ant Fly*
Photo courtesy Ascent Fly Fishing

Figure 19 *Red Ant Fly*
Photo courtsey Ascent Fly Fishing

*"I suspect that a sense of humor
is the most valuable thing
an angler can own."*

~ Jim Harrison ~

The 1924 Collection: XII—The Silver Sedge

As an introduction to those who don't know, the word "sedge" derives from the fact that adult Caddis flies can often be seen hanging on to sedge grass near the water's edge.

As it's a reliable winner, I have a great fancy for this fly and consider it quite the best standby for the hot months of July and August. I have heard it said that it will work exceptionally well in hot weather when the fish are smutting.

Some fly fishers insist the Silver Sedge can be fished in any position on the cast from the start of the mayfly period through the end of the season.

The Silver Sedge is a proven warrior, a traditional trout fly that has stood the test of time for over 100 years. This fly is a good impersonation of the many small, light-colored sedges of the dog days of summer.

Our friends at *www.frankiemcphillips.com*[7] give us this hint for how to use the Silver Sedge effectively:

Whilst dry flies are commonly fished static, sedge patterns such as the Murrough, Grey Flag, Shellin, Melvin, and Small Brown Sedge are best retrieved with short pulls to represent the characteristic skittering motion of the natural sedge across the water surface.

No doubt about it—this Silver Sedge is a must-have in any serious fly fisher's box.

Figure 20 *Silver Sedge*
Photo courtsey www.fishingfliesandlures.com

---

7 *Copy courtesy frankiemcphillips.com, with our sincere thanks.*

The 1924 Collection: XIII—The Cinnamon Ant

This is also an August ant fly and is very deadly when it appears. It can be used all through August and September and is particularly useful in the late afternoon and the early evening.

No less an authority than The English Fly Fishing Shop[8] opined this:

> The Cinnamon Caddis is an ideal pattern to imitate the lighter winged caddis you find hatching around dusk.
>
> Rainbow and Brown trout feel more secure with the fading light and feed with enthusiasm on the newly hatched caddis floating on the surface film, waiting for their wings to dry before they fly for the first time.

So the wise angler stocks up on Cinnamon Ant flies. Summer days are always right around the corner, and a summer dinner of hard-fought trout brought forth with a Cinnamon Ant fly, even more special.

Figure 21 *Cinnamon Ant fly*
Photo courtesy Sportsman's News with our thanks!

8 *Copy courtesy The English Fly Fishing Shop with our thanks!*

The 1924 Collection: XIV—The White Moth

The time for using this fly is at dusk and after on a summer evening. It is particularly useful during heavy hatches at night. May through September are the peak months for this fly, but it can be used with success April through September, with emphasis on those hot summer months.

As the White Moth is a very conspicuous object, you can hardly fail to see when it is on, and then you cannot do without it.

Finally, some fly fishers fish this fly dry in teams of two, about 4 to 6 feet apart. As mentioned earlier, when discussing sedge flies, they are best retrieved with short pulls to represent the natural skittering motion of the natural sedge across the water's surface.

Figure 22 *White Moth Fly*
Photo courtsey www.fish-fishingflies.co.uk

The 1924 Collection: XV—The Royal Coachman

The Royal Coachman is probably the most recognized fly in all of the fly fishing world. One will find this humble little fly adorning hats, shirts, mugs, and artworks.

A classic British fly, to be sure, we find the origins of the Coachman fly attributed to Mr. Tom Bosworth, a nineteenth-century fly fisherman, Englishman, and fly tier. He was a coachman and drove coaches for three British monarchies. Although by his occupation he was, de facto and de jure, a "royal coachman," he chose to call his fly simply a "Coachman."

Royal or not, this is another great favorite of mine for evening and night fishing.

What the trout take it for I do not know, for there is nothing which it exactly resembles. But take it they do. Possibly because, in the dusk, the contrast between the dark body and the white wings enables them readily to perceive it.

There are several variants of this fly. Whatever they may be, Royal Coachman flies continue to be favored by trout—even finicky ones!

Figure 23 *The Royal Coachman*
Photo courtsey www.flyshack.com

The 21st Century Collection and a Column

Trout and the insects they eat live on a different time scale from the average fisherman. Their clock is geologic.

Ours is the short blur of a lifetime measured as the Bible says in *Psalm 90:10*, "The years of our life are seventy; or even by reason of strength eighty; ... and they are soon gone." Seventy years is only a little over 25,000 sunrises.

Although not a truly fair comparison, the species of fish we call trout have seen millions.

So logically, it follows that trout have been eating many (but not all, to be sure) of the same grub for eons. A mayfly of the year 454 B.C. looked like a mayfly of the 21st Century.

That said, and before we get into our list of flies of today, we would be amiss if we didn't point out two crucial differences between fly fishing in the 21st Century and fly fishing in 1920:

How flies are presented to fish *has* changed. Drastically.

Strike indicators are of terrific value when searching water columns and detecting strikes. Move them up or down on your leader as an aid in controlling the depth of your drift. Xink or split shots help you get your fly down the vertical column. Xink is especially useful where split shot is illegal or if you want just a small amount of sink.

Casting placement affects your depth as well; the further upstream you cast gives your fly more time to sink before hitting the part of the drift you are working. Fly weight is important as well. Bead heads obviously add weight to standard nymphs and streamers. And certain patterns like Copper John or others made of wire are heavier. Line choice also has an obvious impact.

The net-net (if you'll forgive the pun) is that adjustments can be made throughout the day as needed or through different sections of water to move your fly up or down through the water column as you see fit. Or as the fish teach you.

If you have nothing to go on, try starting with the middle column, and gradually go deeper until you find fish or until your visual cues tell you something different.

Now, let's discuss how the nature of fly fishing flies has changed in the last 100 years.

Flies of Today

Today flies fall roughly into these groups: dry flies, wet flies (including nymphs), streamers, poppers, and terrestrials.

Let's look at each in turn.

Dry Flies are what most people think of today (and in 1924) when going fly fishing. Dry flies are fished on or at the surface of the water. Additionally, as a rule, they mimic adult or emerging insects such as mayflies, grasshoppers, caddisflies, stoneflies, midges, and damselflies. Dry flies are designed to "match the hatch"; that is, to closely resemble the types of insects that hatch from the nymph stage into flying insects.

This class of flies is by and large not all that different than back in 1924 save this: the materials used to construct them are radically different today versus back then. That said, today's new materials do the same thing as the natural furs and feathers of yesteryear—they serve the same purpose, that of imitating something in nature. A century ago, flies were made out of natural components because artificial fabrics, human made furs, and other contemporary fly tying ingredients had not been invented yet.

To dry fly purists (the majority of fly fishers?), dry flies are as good as it gets. The logic here is that with dry (surface) flies, the fish's take is visual. As such, the onus is on the fly fisher for accurate casting and subtle presentation. Medium- to slow-action rods put dry flies on the water more delicately than faster action rods. Ironically for a book whose content spans 100 years—back to the era in which bamboo rods were highly prized—today's dry fly anglers prefer... bamboo rods.

Wet Flies (which includes the class of flies known as **nymphs**) are, as the name implies, fished below the water's surface. This makes sense as most fish feed 80+% of the time underwater.

The bulk of wet flies are tied to imitate natural creatures such as pupal- and nymph-stage aquatic insects, shrimp, fish eggs, worms, and crayfish.

With wet flies, the strike of the fish occurs under the surface of the water. This presents a challenge for the fly fisher: to "see" (some say sense or "feel") the strike by either watching for fly line movement or by watching for fish to flash underwater. We will discuss this more in a later chapter.

Many anglers avoid this "feel" issue through the use of a "strike indicator." If you've ever used a bobber when fishing for bass or crappie, you have a good grounding in the use of a strike indicator. It's a small float (think: bobber) or a floating feather-like item which you attach some distance up your leader and above the fly. The strike indicator floats on the surface as your fly drifts along underwater. When a fish takes the fly, the indicator can do a few different things. It will either stop, slow down, move upstream, or make some other slightly different action that is not normal.

As useful as this sounds, and it can be most helpful, one must practice intently to master the strike indicator. The main difficulty is learning how to handle the lag time between when the fish takes the fly until you notice the strike indicator move. To truly master fly fishing today, this is a technique you should take the time to learn.

Streamers as a lure are based on a simple assumption: that larger fish need more food and therefore eat larger prey. As such, streamers are outsized wet flies created to mimic larger prey such as large insects, baitfish, leeches, crayfish, or even small animals.

Streamers are fished somewhat differently than a "typical" wet or dry fly. When one thinks of fishing a streamer, one should use the same technique one would use to fish a lure. That is to say, the intrepid fly fisherperson retrieves, or strips, the streamer back in a way meant to imitate prey.

As a rule-of-thumb, one need not be concerned with "feeling" a fish hit a streamer. Strikes on streamers are typically hard. You know when a fish has hit it.

Poppers typically have an angled, blunt, or scoop face. Sometimes called surface lures, and a direct descendent of surface lures used in topwater bass fishing, poppers are fished on the surface of the water.

They are typically retrieved with quick strips interrupted with twitches. This action is intended to mimic wounded baitfish, frogs, mice, and other small prey animals.

Terrestrials form the last group of flies. Strictly speaking, terrestrials may be called wet, dry, or even streamer flies by purists. We have broken them out as a separate topic merely for simplicity's sake.

A grasshopper, for example, is obviously a terrestrial with which you are familiar. So are red or black ants. Beetles are clearly terrestrial. As our friends at Orvis[9] put it:

> Trout feed on terrestrials throughout most of the prime angling season, particularly during the late summer months as they blunder into streams and other water.
>
> Likewise, hoppers and crickets—among many fishes' favorite forage—often end up in rivers through late summer and early fall.

If you enjoy fishing in small streams, terrestrials are even more important than in larger rivers. This is due to the fact that a trout's diet in (some) small streams is composed mainly of terrestrials because streams of this size do not have expanses of insect-producing riffles.

Also, note that terrestrials can be more productive on windy days and all day long when terrestrial insects are active and more likely to fall into a river.

Very well, then. We have explained the various families of most flies used today. Now let's get down to the list we've compiled of 21 of today's most productive flies.

The List

In the "Recommended Flies of the 21st Century" section to follow, you'll see us reference primarily dry, wet, and terrestrial flies.

Having just explained the leading families of flies, why didn't we include streamers and poppers? Our logic is this: this book is called *First Steps to Fly Fishing*. As such, we kept our list targeted to the basics of fly fishing: wet flies (including nymphs), dry flies, and terrestrials.

Assembling this list was no trivial task. We consulted the Internet and compiled data and input from no fewer than six "best flies" lists for a start, including listings from such esteemed sources as *Field and Stream* magazine and Orvis.

Now we know fly fisherpersons who might argue strenuously as to other flies they think should also belong on this list. That is just fine

---

9 Copy courtesy *www.orvis.com*, with our thanks!

with us. Because while many folks may have many ideas for additional flies, everyone should agree that the flies we have chosen are *valid and productive.*

We intend to get you into your first steps in productive and enjoyable fly fishing, not to keep you locked up in a fly fishing store comparing flies.

And as we mentioned, there are (and probably always have been and will be) fashions in fly fishing.

On to the list!

The 21ˢᵗ Century Fly List (in alphabetical order)

1) Adams
2) Ant
3) Blue Winged Olive
4) Copper John
5) Eggs
6) Elk Hair Caddis
7) Grasshopper
8) Griffith's Gnat
9) Hare's Ear
10) Parachute Adams
11) Pheasant Tail
12) Prince Nymph
13) Royal Coachman
14) Royal Wulff
15) Rusty Spinner
16) Sparkle Dun
17) Stimulator
18) WD-40
19) Woolly Bugger
20) Zebra Midge

The 21st Century Fly Collection:
#1 — Adams

As abstracted from Mr. James Jolie and the blog at *www.riverbum.com*[10]:

> The Adams fly is around a century old. It is unquestionably one of the top-selling dry fly patterns of all time.
>
> Mr. Leonard Halladay is credited with designing the original pattern for the Adams fly in 1922 and named the pattern after his fly fishing buddy Mr. Charles Adams. However, the actual mayfly the Adams is supposed to represent remains a mystery. It matches several species exceptionally well and is very "buggy" in its design. Word quickly spread, orders for the Adams kept coming in, and the rest is history.
>
> The fly has changed some over the years, but the basic pattern has remained. The wool included in the original design has been changed out to muskrat fur to increase buoyancy. In the 1930s, the wing pattern changed from being closer and angled forward over the head, to a posture that is now more upright and separated. Sometime later, the tail was altered from golden pheasant to a mix of grizzly and hackle.
>
> Over the years, other variations have been made to this ubiquitous fly. There's a female version—featuring bright yellow imitating the egg sack. There a parachute version, an irresistible version, and even one called "Purple Haze," which is an Adams dry fly substituting purple thread for grey.
>
> The Adams fly is one for the ages. I would seriously doubt that there is a dry fly box in America that doesn't contain this fly.

Figure 24 *Adams fly*
Photo courtesy Trident Fly Fishing

10 Much thanks, to Mesa, AZ-based RiverBum!

The 21st Century Fly Collection:
#2 — Ant (Black, Red, Cinnamon)

The ant is proof that good things come in exceedingly small packages. Few serious fly fishers attend the water without a selection of ant flies to choose from.

Abstracted from a post by Mr. Craig Moore and the blog at *flyfishusa.com*[11]:

> Reportedly, ants are the most numerous of all insects. They have only one or two queens per colony, so when a new queen is born, that queen has to leave and start its colony.
>
> Since ants are so numerous, their "hatches" are of significant importance to the angler in nearly every environment that contains insect-eating fish. Carpenter ants are most notable because of their large size but are only one of many ant migrations that occur in the U.S.
>
> For example, the next time you are fishing a stream in the desert, take a moment and examine how many kinds of ants inhabit even that barren landscape. You will see a multitude of sizes and colors. Most ants seem to forage around water. As such, some ants do fall in the water. Ants are clumsy fliers and weak swimmers. So they don't stay on the surface of the water for very long before they drown and sink. Fishing an ant pattern as a wet fly can be very productive any time the weather is warm, but especially during or just after a queen migration.
>
> As mentioned, in many sections of the U.S., "terrestrial-insect-fall" is a significant food source for native trout in mountain streams and lakes. Ant hatches happen when the air temperature climbs above 85 degrees for the first time during the spring or summer season. While hatch timing can vary drastically with elevation or climatic changes, expect to see carpenter ant queen flights through the April-to-August time frame.
>
> The ants I've seen vary significantly in size from approximately 3/32" to 3/4" Most ant bodies are very dark—brown, gray, or black. Some ants are reddish-brown (red and "cinnamon" colored ants), while others have black and red parts. The average sizes of flies to match most of the different ant species I've encountered are #16, #14, #12, and #10.
>
> Real ants are very hard to see on the water, even winged ants.

11 Thanks to The Fly Fishing Shop – they built *flyfishusa.com*. Thanks again!

Some ant dry flies are dressed with white or colored wing material to make them easier to see in adverse light conditions. Today's wing materials are easily colored with a waterproof felt marker to help give you an even greater edge. We suggest you carry dark gray and brown markers.

Be sure to carry a selection of winged and wingless ant patterns in black and red (reddish) colors to cover a variety of situations. Floating ant dry flies can be effective search patterns for a host of fish species.

Figure 25 *Red Ant Fly*
Photo courtesy Ascent Fly Fishing

Figure 26 *Black Ant Fly*
Photo courtesy Ascent Fly Fishing

The 21ˢᵗ Century Fly Collection:
#3 — Blue Winged Olive

Blue Winged Olive (BWO) trout flies may be small in size, but they are significant to the fly fisher. Large and trophy-sized trout sip these little but numerous mayflies in fishing spots across the world.

In the abstract, our friends at *www.perfectflystore.com*[12] describe these beauties this way:

> The BWO nymphs are members of the *Baetidae* family. They are free swimmers who vary in color from dark brown to light olive or emerald. All of them are slim, minnow-like nymphs. BWO nymphs exist in all types of trout streams and are one of the most abundant species of aquatic insects.
>
> Several slightly different species hatch at various times throughout the year, and BWOs act more like minnows than crawler or clinger nymphs. They can and do cling tightly to rocks and the stems of plants when they feed in current.
>
> The nymphs emerge in the water's surface skim, but trout will eat them well before they emerge and eat them below the surface as they rise to the surface to hatch.
>
> Let's now turn our attention to presentation.
>
> One method of fishing the BWO nymph is to use a small strike indicator placed about 16 to 20 inches above your fly. As an alternative, you can also use a larger dry fly to suspend small BWO nymph imitations, if you prefer. You can also fish BWOs without a strike indicator. That is the way we prefer to fish them. We usually add a small amount of weight a few inches above the fly.
>
> We use both an up-and-across cast and a down-and-across cast depending on the type of water we're fishing. The up and the down presentation is **upstream from the fish** and generally within a 20 to 40-foot range. In the up-and-across cast, cast the BWO directly in front of your position, and allow the line to drift in a sweeping motion across the stream. The BWO nymph will sink during the first part of the sweep, then rise at the end. Strip the line slowly upstream at the end of the sweep, and watch for a strike. During the retrieve, try dropping your rod tip down. This action may stimulate activity as the BWO fly drops down and moves backward. The down-and-across method works more or less the same except you are casting directly across the water, perpendicular to the flow, and allowing the line to drift in a sweep across the stream.
>
> As a general rule, in rough pocket water, use the up-and-across cast placed at the end of the current seams. In the smooth flowing water, use a down-and-across cast.

---

12 *Copy courtesy www.perfectflystore.com* **with our profound thanks!**

The early season hatches usually start as early as noon and can hatch until 4:00 or 5:00 PM. It is a good idea to fish a BWO nymph imitation in the mornings before the hatch. And, it's often a good idea to just go ahead and fish the BWO nymph imitation during the time they are hatching.

If you are fishing waters where populations of BWOs occur, and there's no visible hatch occurring at the time, it may be wise to fish the BWO nymph. Use a strike indicator and perhaps some added weight of appropriate size for the depth and current of the water you are dealing with.

That is also a useful search pattern to use during the hours preceding a hatch. That said, in the earliest part of a hatch, you may have better success fishing the BWO below a BWO emerger or dry fly pattern. The BWO nymphs usually work even when BWO flies are emerging. Trout seem to prefer eating the BWO nymphs just before they emerge.

Remember, trout feeding on these small mayflies are not going to go to a lot of trouble to eat them. They don't need to.

So, generally speaking, you can avoid the rougher, faster, more turbulent waters and concentrate on the smoother water because that is what the trout will be doing.

Figure 27 *Blue WInged Olive (BWO) fly.*
Photo courtesy Trident Fly Fishing

Figure 29 *Blue Wing Oliver (BWO) Emerger*
Photo courtesy Mid-Hudson Trout Unlimited

"To be consistently successful in his pursuit of the various game fish is, the all-around fly angler must be at least amateur entomologist, ichthyologists, and meteorologist."

~ Tom McNally ~

The 21st Century Fly Collection: #4 — Copper John

The Copper John is one of the most widely used, widely respected, and most dependable flies on the water today. We are fortunate to have a Copper John expert available to us, Mr. Car1l Haensel. He wrote a very sound piece on *www.fishandboat.com*[13], and we are lucky enough to abstract it here for you today.

Created by well-known fly designer John Barr of Colorado, this fly not only is good in Western rivers, but it has also produced fish in just about every location that it's been cast. This pattern is shaped like a large clinging mayfly or small stonefly. Its two goose tails look just like the tails of a stonefly.

Fishing this fly in fast water is a great way to start using it. Try using it as the lead fly in a two- or three-fly combination rig. The weight of the fly will help get it down fast. The flash of this pattern is more likely to catch fish in water where the fish have less time to analyze the fly. It often doesn't need any additional weight to get it down to the fish, which can make a multiple fly rig much easier to fish.

Fish this pattern on a dead drift, and swing it up at the end of your drift, as you would fish other nymphs. Even with a heavy fly such as this, make sure to use enough weight to get it down to the bottom of the run. Nymphs floating two feet over a trout's head in fast water are rarely effective. This fly also can be an effective still-water pattern. Try fishing it in a count-down method. Then use a varied retrieve until you find a style that starts to hook fish. If you've not done it before, cast your fly out and count slowly until you begin your retrieve. If you're successful, you can replicate the same cast again. If you don't get anything, try a longer count to get your fly deeper.

After your countdown, strip the fly line in as slowly as you can bear, without snagging the fly on the bottom. As your stripping hand nears your reel, make a sharp jerk with your wrist toward your body. Then begin your slow strip again. This mimics the locomotion of many different insects.

Anglers can buy Copper Johns in a wide range of colors that can imitate most of the hues of small stoneflies and mayflies. Wherever you travel, bring a few Copper Johns along.

---

13 *Copy courtesy www.fishandboat.com, by Carl Haensel, with our grateful thanks!*

Figure 29 *Copper John*
Photo courtesy *www.olefloridaflyshop.com*

"It is always been my private conviction that any person who puts their intelligence up against a fish and loses it had it coming."

~ John Steinbeck ~

The 21st Century Fly Collection:
#5 — Eggs

Fly Fisherperson purists will argue that fishing eggs is, strictly speaking, not "fly" fishing.

Granted. Mea culpa. We concede.

But if you want to catch fish, forget about subtleties. Eggs catch fish for the same reason you like a couple of hen's eggs sunny-side up—they are amazingly good, and good for you, food.

Even trout know that. So does Nick DelVecchio[14] over at *www.theflycrate.com*. He wrote an excellent piece about fishing with eggs, and we are fortunate to be able to abstract it here for you.

Many associate gaudy, articulated streamers with big trout, but it's often eggs that yield the true giants of the deep.

Pound for pound, nothing has more protein in a trout's diet than an egg. If there is a chance that fish (of any species) are spawning in a given waterway, odds are our quarry will be keying on eggs. Anglers should have an arsenal of egg flies on deck and ready throughout the season to capitalize on what trout like best!

Here's how to fly fish egg flies and some of our favorite egg fly patterns for winter trout or fall steelhead.

Getting the color and size of an egg fly is just as important as it is with mayflies and midges. Good starting points are orange and light pink, with tweaks being made throughout the day. One of the great things about eggs is how easy they are to tie.

Something that egg tiers like to do is an experiment in different volumes of material. The opacity of the flies results in different "looks" of the fly in the water and, thus, more options for the days when fish are picky.

When the egg bite is on, a standard nymph rig might consist of two or three eggs below some weight. In this situation the brighter, and larger, egg is typically tied on first with a smaller fly trailing behind. One of the best trailing flies is a single egg in orange, pink, or cream color. It's so light that even with weight above the point fly, the single egg plays in the current in an almost weightless manner. This is important because, despite their high protein density, fish eggs weigh virtually nothing and move throughout the water freely. Therefore, remember to add enough weight above or below it to get it down where the fish are. If you're looking to add just a single egg to your nymphing rig and not add any additional weight, having a beaded egg is incredibly useful.

14 *Copy courtesy Nick DelVecchio, posting on www.theflycrate.com, with our most sincere thanks!*

Fishing eggs can be somewhat different than conventional nymph rigs. In some ways, specific trout can be pinpointed feeding on eggs just like they can sipping mayflies. Look for trout hanging below spawning fish. If these fish are moving to the left or right aggressively, it is a sign that they are feeding on eggs. An important note is to try not to fish over spawning fish, but rather the ones downstream feeding on eggs.

Once a fish is targeted, use short drifts with a lot of weight landing the flies right below the spawning fish. If done well, our offerings should sink fast and go right past trout feeding below.

Some of the best trophy trout anglers will say that it isn't sculpins or mice that catch the biggest fish, it is eggs. Eggs can consistently be in a waterway and provide a steady stream of calories that make it worthwhile for fish of all sizes to feed!

While eggs are great fishing year-round, you'll notice a big difference during the spawning seasons. When looking at the breeding seasons below, you won't be fishing these exact species. In fact, you will be fly fishing the other fish that gather below the breeding grounds to feed on loose eggs that drift downstream. Just commit these seasons to memory as a guideline when eggs will be hot and abundant.

- Carp spawn from April to June in the shallow waters.
- Brook trout spawn from September into October.
- Brown trout spawn from October through December.
- Rainbow trout spawn from February through May.

Please keep in mind not to cast near, wade near, or fish spawning trout. These breeding fish are producing the next generation of trophy trout. They don't need the added stress or exhaustion of human interference.

Figure 30 *Peach Egg pattern*
Photo courtesy www.theflycrate.com

Figure 31 *Beaded Egg Fly*
Photo courtesy www.theflycrate.com

"I do not know anything more beautiful in nature than the head-and-tailing trout."

~ Harry Plunket-Green ~

The 21ˢᵗ Century Fly Collection:
#6 — Elk Hair Caddis

The Elk Hair Caddis is one of the best, most productive, and most useful dry flies of all time.

Some of their best work occurs when caddis are laying eggs. However, this fly shines as an attractor/searching fly, especially during the summer months when the mayflies have slowed. Fish this fly dead-drift or better yet skate it. It also works great with a small dropper off the back.

We abstracted Mr. Jason Akl[15] on *1source.basspro.com/* from a great blog post about fishing this seriously well-revered fly.

Fly anglers have successfully used the Elk Hair Caddis to catch multiple species of fish. Trout have to be top on this list as they seem the most eager to chase high floating dry flies.

The great success of this pattern might be due to the widespread nature of caddis flies. Still, I like to believe it is because of the unique arrangement of the hackle, in combination with the elk hair wing, which allows this fly to ride high and dry on the water's surface. If you compare the actual design of the elk hair fly pattern to a real-life caddis fly, the profile (from below) and the action are quite similar.

When caddis flies sit on the water, you see only the wings. Even from below, the profile comes from how the wings tent over the body and rest on the water's surface. The elk hair tied onto the top of the hook shank and squared off at the head do a great job recreating this wing profile.

In addition to this, caddis flies just do not sit in the water's surface. They jump, bounce and skitter across the surface, enticing fish into biting. The body of the elk hair caddis allows the fly to sit high on top of the water surface but also allows the fly to skate/bounce when the fly line is lifted lightly.

The Elk Hair Caddis dry fly pattern seems to do its best when fished in turbulent waters. The thick elk hair wings, along with the hackle body, allow the fly to avoid getting dragged under even in the rougher flows. If you plan on fishing slower waters, it is best to clip the body hackle flat alongside the underbody so that fly will ride lower on the water's surface.

To fish the elk hair caddis patterns, use standard dry fly presentations and target fast water seams, or slow pools adjacent to fast water.

If you are in a section of the stream that has lots of vegetation, try targeting spots near overgrown banks, below overhanging trees, and in or around other bank vegetation.

Watching fish rise to dry flies for me is one of the most exciting ways to fish for trout. The elk hair caddis is a pattern that will undoubtedly attract a fish's interest—and the bite won't be far behind.

---

15 From a post by Jason Akl in 2014 on *https://1source.basspro.com/* with our best thanks!

Figure 32 *Elk Hair Caddis*
Photo courtesy Big Horn Flies

"Lo the angler. He is riseth in the morning and upsetteth the whole household. Mighty are his preparations. He goeth forth with great hope in his heart—and when the day is far spent he returneth, smelling of strong drink, and the truth is not in him."

~ Anonymous ~

The 21ˢᵗ Century Fly Collection: #7 — Grasshopper

Grasshoppers are ubiquitous. And since they live alongside rivers and streams, they make a natural bait for fly fishers.

Back in 2017, Dave Goetz, over at *2 Guys And A River*[16] (*www.2guysandariver.com*), wrote the definitive piece on fly fishing grasshoppers. We're fortunate to have an abstraction of that piece to share with you here.

8 Tips for Fly Fishing Grasshoppers

There is no such thing as a grasshopper hatch, of course. Grasshoppers live and die in the riparian zones along rivers and streams.

Here are a few tips to help beginners enjoy grasshoppers when fly fishing:

---

1. Let the river warm up.

Several years ago, in late July, we arrived at a creek about 8:30 or 9 AM, and we rigged up with grasshoppers (hoppers).

Nothing rose to our casts. I became a bit grumpy.

I switched to nymphs for an hour or so, and then I walked upriver where my fishing partner Steve was hauling in his second or third brown on a hopper imitation.

It was like the bell rang some time between 10 and 11 AM, and the trout started feeding on hoppers. It was nonstop until late afternoon. Often, the trout won't begin to hit hoppers until mid- to late-morning, when the vegetation along the banks warms up.

---

2. Big is not bad.

I learned to fly fish in Montana and Colorado, but in recent years, I've spent more days on smaller creeks than I have the big rivers of the West.

I've grown acclimated to the spring-creek requirements of finer tackle and smaller flies. Consequently, I also reach for smaller grasshopper imitations. But, if you're fishing out West, select a bigger hopper just because you can. Go for size 4 or 6. Make sure you have 3X or 4X tippet to handle the bigger bug. And then see what happens.

---

16 *Copy courtesy of Dave Goetz on the blog at https://2guysandariver.com with our very profound thanks!*

3. Don't forget the relaxed sip.

I love the aggressive strikes that hoppers provoke. But not all hopper strikes are aggressive. Some fish prefer to mouth or toy with the hopper. Crazy, I know. I've caught some large cutthroat in Yellowstone National Park by merely being more patient with my hook set. In general, fly fishers, especially those new to the sport, tend to rip the hook out of the mouth of fish. Certainly, trout love to slash at grasshoppers, but there are often more subtle takes as well.

That means being vigilant when you feel or see a take. Some fly fishers repeat a mantra or phrase when they feel a take, such as "God save the Queen" or "The Cubs finally won a World Series!" depending on your country of origin.

Then they set the hook!

4. Give it some action.

Real grasshoppers don't float passively on the water unless they are already dead.

If the wind has blown a hopper into the water, then likely it is kicking for shore. If you're fishing a swift-moving river like the Yellowstone, then you may not need to twitch or skate the hopper. But in more flat stretches, you may want to give the hopper some action by twitching it or skating it across the surface.

5. Drop another terrestrial.

Several years ago, while fishing in Yellowstone Park, I dropped a fat foam flying ant off my top hopper pattern, and I caught more cutthroat off the ant than I did the hopper. I tied the foam ant about nine to twelve inches below the grasshopper, and it worked beautifully.

The Yellowstone River was swift, and with the current, the ant seemed to float just beneath the film. Several times, I watched the shadow of a cutthroat appear from the depths of the river and grab the ant.

6. Pay attention to color.

There are a million varieties of hoppers and a host of different earth-tone hues from green to yellow and to brown.

I've made the mistake of buying hoppers from a fly shop in Montana and wondering why they don't work as well in the spring creeks of the Driftless (southwestern Wisconsin, for example). You'll want to do a little research at your local fly shop. Size and color are essential, and every fly (or hopper!) is local.

7. Throw one on when nothing is rising.

It always strikes me as odd that when nothing is rising, I can throw on a hopper in late summer, and an aggressive trout takes the imitation.

Through the years, I can't remember a time when I've noticed trout rising to hoppers, and then decided to throw on a hopper. The creek runs through a meadow. There are hoppers. And I decide to throw on a hopper. *Voila!* I catch trout on hoppers.

Hoppers promise a gob of calories, and during mid to late summer, trout want the gob.

8. Start with foam.

Most hopper patterns come in three styles: foam, natural, and parachute. I tend to start with foam, though I will use more natural patterns when fishing slower water. The parachute hopper always is a win in riffles—I can see it!

Grasshopper season is like the Christmas season. It comes once a year. And if you can have even one great day fly fishing grasshoppers, you've received the best present of the year.

Figure 33 *Grasshopper fly pattern
Courtsey of Orvis Corp.*

Figure 34 *Foam Body Grasshopper Dry Fly Brown/Tan Body. Courtsey of TheFlyFishingPlace*

"No sport affords a greater field for observation and study than fly fishing, and it is the close attention paid to the minor happenings upon the stream that marks the finished angler."

~ George LaBranche ~

The 21st Century Fly Collection: #8 — Griffith's Gnat

Griffith's Gnat is a reliable choice if you feel like tying your first fly. This little guy is not only a good producer of trout on the line, but they make a superb introduction into tying dry flies.

The Griffith's Gnat mimics a midge cluster, and you should feel free to tie it in a variety of sizes, typically using hooks sizes 14-24.

The Griffith's Gnat seems to get overlooked as fly fishers reach for a more "popular" fly such as a Caddis or a Blue Winged Olive. But many a fly fisher also knows that the Griffith's Gnat can be quite productive when other flies just aren't getting the job done on tailwaters or freestones.

The Griffith's Gnat is a multitalented fly. It can mimic a midge cluster of mating flies, or it can stand duty as a single adult midge—depending on the size you have tied on.

This fly works well as a second fly, trailing off of another dry fly. And experience shows that trout seem to like Griffith's Gnat in slower, flat water when located low in the foam.

The Griffith's Gnat was created by George Griffith, one of the co-founders of Trout Unlimited.

Figure 35 *The Griffith's Gnat.*
Photo courtsey madriveroutfitters.com

Figure 36 *Griffith's Gnat dry fly.*
Photo courtsey selectafly.com

*"Most fishermen swiftly
learn that it's a pretty good rule
never to show a favorite spot to
any fishermen you wouldn't
trust with your wife."*

~ Robert Traver ~

The 21st Century Fly Collection: #9 — Hare's Ear (aka Gold Ribbed Hare's Ear Nymph (GRHE))

When we selected the flies for this list, this particular creation was on everyone's list as a "must have" fly. The Gold Ribbed Hare's Ears may be a mouthful to say, but its reputation for catching fish well precedes it.

The well-written blog at *www.theessentialfly.com/blog/*[17] had a very nice piece on this elegant fish warrior, which we abstracted for you here:

Possibly one of the most essential fishing flies ever tied is the Gold Ribbed Hare's Ear Nymph (GRHE). If you examine every fly fisher's fly box world-wide, regardless of species that they are targeting, the GRHE would probably be one, if not the most prolific fly you would find. If you confined your consideration only to trout fly fisherman, then the certainty of finding the GRHE approaches near certainty.

GRHE is perhaps the most recognized, fished, and proven nymph ever tied or purchased. The Gold Ribbed Hare's Ear's texture and colors, like game cock soft hackles, gold tinsel ribbing, and cock pheasant tail fibers, convey a superbly 'buggy' outline. And make for a highly 'impressionistic' fly. Impressionistic flies are capable of being viewed by fish as many different 'bugs,' including shrimp or scud, sow bug, sedge pupa, larva, and many mayfly species. Indeed the GRHE can even be viewed as a small fish.

The texture and color of the GRHE can be effectively fished in two different ways. Either imitating a hatching insect near the surface or fished down low in the water to resemble a bug, scud, or shrimp.

Near the surface, fish can see this fly as a pupa in the process of hatching, breaking its exoskeleton, and the residual nymphal skin being discarded.

Using lightweight GRHE on long tapered leaders with a floating line on the surface is ideal for lakes and reservoirs.

On rivers use heavier GRHE or bead-head GRHE flies upstream and dead drift lower in the water where it can be taken by fish to be a shrimp, scud, or other bottom-dwelling feasts for a trout.

The Hare's Ear Nymph will attract fish even when there is no hatch occurring. It imitates almost any natural nymph. I would also suggest you try it in runs and riffles or fish it in still waters. Stripping this nymph back toward you on a lake or pond can get trout on the rod.

---

17 From *"Possibly The Two Most Important Fishing Flies Ever Tied are the Pheasant Tail Nymph and Gold Ribbed Hare's Ear Nymph (GRHE)"on the blog of www.theessentialfly.com with our sincere thanks!*

Figure 37 - *Gold Ribbed Hare's Ear Nymph*
Photo Courtesy www.orvis.com.

*"A spin fisher can fish a river.
A fly fisher must know a river."*

~ Dave Hughes ~

The 21ˢᵗ Century Fly Collection: #10 — Parachute Adams

Another Adams on our list. And, yes, this one does have a direct lineage from its famous ancestor (the Adams)—plus the advantage of a parachute. It is a beautiful dry fly to cast with its bright white post and dark body, making it easily visible in almost all light conditions.

The Parachute Adams is a very versatile attractor fly (more on what that is in just a moment). It can be fished as an imitation of olives, midges, or tricos by merely adjusting the size. Add in a variation of body color (and of sizes, from 12-26 typically), and the Parachute Adams can imitate other bugs as well.

But as mentioned, the Parachute Adams finds its highest service as an attractor fly—fished when no hatch is present, or with no intention of imitating a specific hatch. It no doubt imitates an adult mayfly, which means it mimics an awful lot of small flies. If you skitter it across the water, it can even resemble a Caddis. When spinners are falling, it will fill in nicely for that, too. That's its real power: however you choose to fish it, you should find that it consistently draws the interest of trout young and old.

The modern Parachute Adams and the parachute style of tying have continued to be very popular. They land upright, float well, and, as mentioned, are very visible to the fly fisher (and to the trout!).

As with all attractor flies, the reasoning is vague as to what, exactly, a Parachute Adams suggests to trout. While its traditional gray color most closely resembles the Blue-Winged Olive, its effectiveness, as mentioned earlier, is not limited to that hatch.

Some fly fishers hold the belief that the shape or form of the Parachute Adams, rather than its color, is what makes it attractive to trout. The Parachute Adams lies flush on the water's surface, creating a silhouette not dissimilar to, say, a crippled dun. That spells dinner to a hungry trout.

Figure 38 *Parachute Adams.*
Photo courtsey theflyfisher.com.au.

A man comes into a shop and asks,
"Can I have a rod and
reel for my son?"
The owner replies, "Sorry, sir.
We don't do trades."

~ Anonymous ~

The 21st Century Fly Collection:
#11 — Pheasant Tail

According to flyandlure.org[18]:

> The Pheasant Tail Nymph is a classic fly pattern invented by Frank Sawyer, a famous river keeper on the Hampshire Avon. It's still an effective and widely used fly pattern on both rivers and still waters. It also resembles a wide range of underwater nymphs, so it can work throughout the year.
>
> While Sawyer's original pattern was tied with only two materials, pheasant tail and copper wire, modern variations of the design have evolved this fly into a range of related patterns.
>
> Sawyer is said to have designed this fly to imitate several species of the Baetis family, generally referred to as the "olives." In streams and rivers, the Pheasant Tail can be presented below the surface if required. Still, it shows its real magic when an angler lets the fly sink close to the riverbed on a dead drift, and then *gently* raises the fly in the water to imitate the behavior of a natural insect.
>
> This behavior of the fly stimulates trout to regard the fly as natural food and to try to eat it, at which point the hook can be set. According to Wikipedia, "This technique has become known as the 'Induced Take.'" The development of this technique may be considered to be as important as the development of the fly itself.

To fish the Pheasant Tail, cast upstream and allow the current to present your fly naturally. Alternatively, cast across the stream, let the fly sink, and, as the fly approaches feeding trout, stop the line and allow the fly to rise in the water. Watch the trout if you can, or watch the tip of the fly line for any movement and, if seen, lift the rod tip, slowly whisper to yourself, "We the People of the United States," and gently set the hook.

On lakes, the Pheasant Tail is a very successful fly in mid-day during the *Callibaetis* season. Try employing a floating line with a greased sunken leader, and then retrieve the fly very slowly and just below the surface. Pay particular attention to shallow areas near weed beds. Again, watch the tip of the fly line for any movement and, if seen, lift the rod tip, slowly whisper to yourself, "In order to form a more perfect Union," and then gently set the hook.

The Pheasant Tail will have done its work!

---

18 *With our thanks, Fly and Lure!*

Figure 39 *The Pheasant Tail fly.*
Photo courtsey www.theessentialfly.com

"Never go fishing with someone else's kid unless you enjoy kids a lot more than you do fishing."

~ John Gierach ~

The 21st Century Fly Collection: #12 — Prince Nymph

No less a venerable source than the Orvis Corporation says this about this well-respected fly: "The Prince Nymph is easily ranked one of the top 10 fly fishing nymphs of all time along with the Hare's Ear and the Pheasant Tail."

It has a very well-defined profile that is unmistakable, and fish take it with abandon. Generally used in fast water, these nymphs are an attractor that can draw strikes anywhere and can be used in warm water as well. Sizes typically range from 8 to 16. The Prince Nymph pattern is also tied (or purchased) in larger sizes such as 6-12 for steelhead. This fly is often weighted using a bead head and/or lead-free wire.

Designed initially as a stonefly imitation, the Prince Nymph (also known by some fly fishers as the Brown Forked Tail) doesn't look exactly like, well, anything. Nevertheless, in this case, being "generalized" can be a plus. It means that the Prince Nymph can be useful in a wide variety of situations where you need a fly that can mimic, say, a stonefly, a sowbug, a backswimmer, or some other aquatic insect.

Drift the Prince Nymph along the bottom of fast rivers as a stonefly imitation. Or, retrieve it slowly through ponds as a backswimmer imitation. Alternatively, you can also drift it further up the water column as an emerging mayfly or caddisfly. Use your imagination!

Figure 40 *The Prince Nymph.*
Photo courtsey www.kingfisherflyshop.com

The 21ˢᵗ Century Fly Collection: #13 — Royal Coachman

This fly is such a classic. We had to include it here. Please see the listing in the 1924 fly list section for a complete description.

The 21ˢᵗ Century Fly Collection: #14 — Royal Wulff

The Royal Wulff is a popular artificial fly rendered in an attractor pattern. It is a descendant of both the Royal Coachman fly and the Wulff style of hair wing flies.

The Royal Wulff is a staple in anglers' fly boxes around the world. Fly fisher and writer John Gierach believes the Royal Wulff is one of the most popular dry fly patterns of the last 75 years.

This red, bug-like dry fly uses its attractor design to imitate many different types of mayflies and terrestrials. A great dry fly for prospecting a promising stretch of water, the Royal Wulff can be fished in slow or fast water. Typically, in freshwater, this fly is worked in sizes 10-18.

As our friends at Duranglers of Durango, Colorado, put it, "It works. Plain and simple."

Figure 41 *Royal Wulff.*
Photo courtsey www.duranglers.com

The 21ˢᵗ Century Fly Collection:
#15 — Rusty Spinner

Take these three things: a river (typically), a mayfly (preferably both real and tied), and a fisherperson. Much of dry-fly fishing for trout over the centuries has been reduced to these common denominator elements.

And if as a fly fisher, your choice of a tied mayfly imitator was the Rusty Spinner, there's an excellent chance you'll have a good day on your choice of water.

The most common refrain I heard when researching the Rusty Spinner was: "It just works!"

If you forgive me a minor science detour, I will explain: Immediately after spawning, a male mayfly will fall to the water, spread its wings wide, and die. Likewise, upon depositing its eggs in the water, a female mayfly will also pass away, and spread its wings wide. Both end up floating on the surface of the water where trout see their outline. Thus the scene is set for a trout feast. A spawned-out mayfly, floating on top of the water just before and after death, is among the easiest food and fastest calories available for feeding trout.

And the Rusty Spinner is, you guessed it, tied to match the look of the low floating profile of a spawned out mayfly spinner.

The fish will take care of the rest.

There isn't much point in delving into how to fish one of these flies: just send it upstream and let the water carry it down or down and across the water.

Finally, there is one thing to consider: as said above, this can be a good earner, so remember to match the fish you're after to the size of the Rusty Spinner you're using. Some people swear that using something as big as a #10 or #12 is perfect during March Brown and Hendrickson season and that fishing something as small as #18 hits the jackpot when the calendar turns to Sulphurs and Olives.

Figure 42 *A Rusty Spinner fly*
Photo courtsey Orvis Corp.

*"Slapping at the fly on your face,
is one of the methods for
unhooking the fish."*

~ President Herbert Hoover ~

The 21st Century Fly Collection:
#16 — Sparkle Dun

This is a unique fly. I have yet to discuss the fly with anyone who doesn't say, "It's great" or some variation of that endorsement. For that reason, I'm going to use the voices of a veteran fly fisher and that of the fly fishing industry to sum up why you want to fish with this fly.

To start, our friends at Orvis have a very concise summary of this fly:

A perfect trout dry fly to imitate many different natural mayflies, including Pale Morning Duns, Sulphur, and Baetis mayflies. The dry fly is sparse, yet gives a great drift. The deer hair lets you track the dry fly. Trout can't resist a Sparkle Dun.

Well—that is a pretty solid start:

✓ "A perfect trout dry fly..."
✓ "...imitate many different natural mayflies..."
✓ "Trout can't resist a Sparkle Dun."

A fly fisher I encountered on the web had this recommendation:

Year after year, if there's one dry fly that out-produces any other dry fly in my box, it's some version, size, or color of the Sparkle Dun.

And Blue Ribbon Flies, a notoriously difficult group of folks to please easily, said this about the Sparkle Dun:

This is the granddaddy of them all. The Sparkle Dun has been responsible for fooling more trout than you could ever count over the last three-plus decades. It is our ultimate confidence pattern. When trout are feeding on emerging mayflies, you'd be hard-pressed to find a better imitation, and it is the first fly we tie on more often than not. If you haven't tried it, you are missing out!

Well—how can I beat those recommendations? You should move directly to your nearest web browser, locate an online fly fishing store, and get yourself several Sparkle Duns today!

Figure 43 *Sparkle Dun*
Photo courtsey Blue Ribbon Flies. Inc.

"...wild trout will take almost any fly, in the educated trout will take only those that imitate in color an action their natural food as they see it."

~ Lee Wulf ~

The 21st Century Fly Collection:
#17 — Stimulator

The Stimulator dry fly is in what some might say a unique position in the world of fly fishing. To start, it is a highly rated fly when employed as an attractor dry fly, mainly when fishing during a stonefly hatch or salmon fly hatch.

Additionally, it also has the reputation of looking so much like a "bug" that it is reputed to be an excellent selection to use as in attractor dry fly pattern when one is "prospecting" for trout—*when there is no hatch*. How does it do that? By resembling many things a trout might wish to sup on while simultaneously imitating nothing in particular.

Fish like that.

This fly comes in a variety of colors and sizes (8-12 being quite popular), which help it look like a black stonefly, a yellow stonefly, a brown stonefly...

Well, you get the idea.

When putting the Stimulator to work, always remember to choose the best size Stimulator relative to the hatch. How would you know that on, say, a new piece of water you've never fished before? Either capture an insect to observe its size, or look at the nymph skins left on the rocks and logs around the river and determine the correct size that way.

One last detail: fly fishers like the Stimulator because they can see it easily on the water. It sits high in the water, even when the water is fast. It continues its excellent work by acting as an indicator in front of another dry fly, an emerger, or even a nymph dropper.

Nice.

Figure 44 *Stimulator*
Photo courtesy Orvis Corp

"Fly fishing is like sex, everyone thinks there is more than there is, and that everyone is getting more than their share."

~ Henry Kanemoto ~

The 21ˢᵗ Century Fly Collection:
#18 — WD-40

Most anglers in the central to the western U.S. find space in their spring fly collection for Blue-Winged Olives (BWO or *Baetis*) imitations. The WD-40 is a wet fly that imitates BWO emergers and a variety of aquatic insects trout like to call din-din.

Many trout fishers we know claim the WD-40 as their "must have" fly, *especially* when trout get picky. Others suggest it as a dropper or tandem fly when fishing tailwater or moving water. Still, others say to use it in freestone stream pools and longer, slower flat runs, from mid- to late summer. On two-fly rigs, you'll often see the WD-40 as the top fly.

According to our friends at Orvis Corporation, "The WD-40 is a very well-liked pattern in the West. It has been around for a while and rightly so—it works. This is an excellent all-around BWO emerger pattern that will imitate several insect species. *Size choice here is critical.*[19]"

Maneuver the WD-40 to the low-to-mid water column for fishing success. Colors are various dark earth tones, and appropriate sizes are 18-22 in most areas. The WD-40 seems to work at all times of the day and can generally be used year-round.

Like the lady fly fisher told me: "The WD-40 works when nothing else does. It's like those old American Express commercials: 'Don't leave home without it!'"

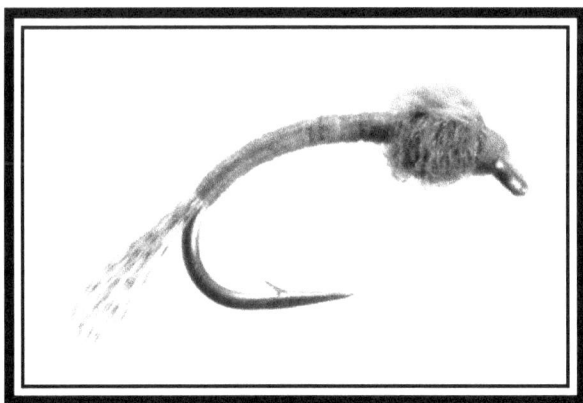

Figure 45 *WD-40 fly*
Photo courtesy Trident Fly Fishing

---

19 *Copy from Orvis Corp. With our thanks. Italic emphasis added.*

Figure 46 *WD-40 in gold color.*
Photo courtesy Orvis Corp

*"One afternoon on the River,
I caught thirty-six inches worth of
trout, in six installments."*

~ Arnold Gingrich ~

The 21ˢᵗ Century Fly Collection: #19 — Woolly Bugger

The Woolly Bugger family of flies is without much doubt probably the most famous, most recognizable, most popular, and the most commonly fished wet fly of all time.

As a wet fly or streamer, it is fished under the water's surface. The woolly bugger has a reputation for working in all kinds of water, including fast water, slow water, rivers (of a certain depth), ponds, and lakes, in dirty water or crystal clear spring-fed creeks, saltwater and freshwater.

It is generally listed as one of the top patterns to have in any fly box, and typically it is fished in sizes 4, 6, 8, and 10. Bead-head Woolly Buggers are also popular.

It imitates crayfish, minnows, leeches, large nymphs, baitfish, drowning terrestrial insects, clamworms, shrimp, crabs, and many other natural foods fish love.

Even a cursory examination of the available writing on this fly tells the same story.

Basically, there isn't a wrong way to fish a Woolly Bugger!

The essence of success, however, seems to be for the fly fisher to select the winning size and color according to each water habitat being fished. And if this sounds a bit like trial-and-error, that's because it is. But with a fly that carries this one's reputation for bringing home the fish—it's a worthwhile trial-and-error.

Figure 47 *Wooly Bugger, Bead Head, in Olive*
Photo courtesy Trident Fly Fishing

The 21ˢᵗ Century Fly Collection:
#20 — Zebra Midge

As you've been reading, fly fishers will run into very opinionated fellow fishers when the discussion turns to which fly is the easiest to fish.

Count the Zebra Midge among the rest, especially if the topic of conversation is the best *tailwater* fly. People swear by it as not only one of the easiest flies to fish—but also one of the easiest flies to tie. If you want to take the first step into fly tying, start with the Zebra.

The Zebra Midge is designed primarily to mimic a midge pupa ascending to the surface of the water to emerge. So, it is most useful to use when you see fish feeding and/or holding high in the water column.

With a fly like the Zebra Midge, you should give some thought to using some form of strike indicator. Especially in active feeding situations where trout may be rising or even breaking the surface to feed, a strike indicator can be beneficial. One such combination might be two of our 21ˢᵗ Century flies: a Zebra Midge and a Parachute Adams. Make sure you adjust your tippit to the depth at which the fish are feeding! (Don't panic if you guess short: fish will move up to take a fly. When unsure, go shorter as a rule of thumb.)

When it's time to cast, try to make the dropper (the Zebra) land upstream of the indicator (the Parachute Adams, in our example). This will assist you in detecting a strike. Trout can be cagey about this. Sometimes the take will be very subtle. That's why some fly fishermen recite a prayer or a quote before trying to set the hook, so the fish has the time to take the hook truly. Sometimes, the take is *so* subtle the indicator won't move even though the fish has taken the dropper!

This is why if you cast above the fish and observe the fish as the indicator/dropper draws near, you might see motion (for example, a quick side-to-side or forward movement followed by the fish remaining in place). This is easy to dismiss as just the fish being wary—but is, in actuality, the fish taking the dropper. Frequently, a trout will see a fly as it is passing and then dart downstream. I'd bet that trout might have your fly.

How do we settle that bet?

WAIT. TO. SET. THE. HOOK.

Stay calm. Wait. Wait again to set the hook. Look for the fish to execute a quick turn to face back into the current (feeding posture to see food coming downstream to it) or abeam of the water (to the side). Such a turn also indicates the fish thinks it snagged a tasty fly, so set the hook!

Figure 48 *Zebra Midge*
Photo courtesy Fly Fish Food on the web

Quite a Selection

There are hundreds of other flies, all of which will kill well at certain times and in certain places. But the list given above will suffice as a basis for the beginning angler. As she grows in the mastery of this fascinating art, she will certainly add to it. And it will not be strange if she forms particular fancies for flies that we have not mentioned.

We all come to have pet flies of our own. One need not be a disciple of Dr. Coue or the Orvis Corporation to recognize that the fly in which we have come fervently to believe is an excellent fly for us. The lists here do not pretend to be complete, still less to be exclusive.

But they are a darn good start to lots of tight lines!

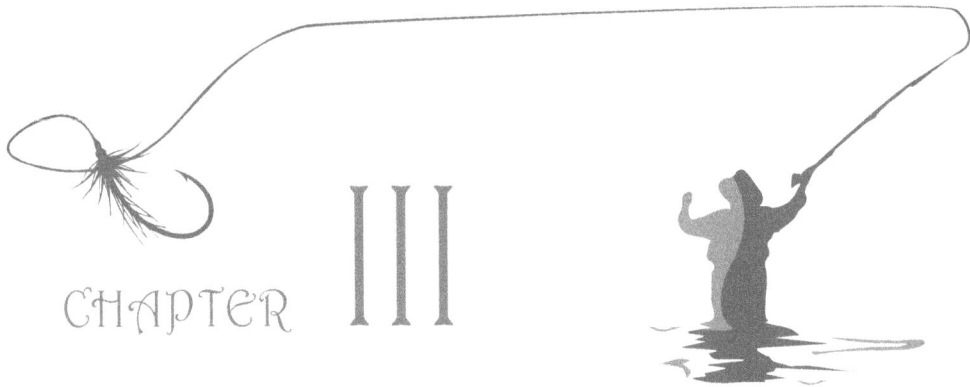

III

How to Fish

(1924 edition, edited)

THE FIRST THING TO learn is how to throw a fly, and you will save yourself a great deal of trouble and disappointment if you acquire the art before and not after you go on your first campaign against the trout.

Have you a lawn?

Capital! Any bit of grass which will give you a length of sixty feet or so is all that is needed. Get an egg or something about the same size—and equally conspicuous—and put it at one end of the lawn.

Editor's Note

*Before we get to actually casting, a critical reminder, please: **always wear eye protection!** A stray line or leader could damage your eyes, with or without a fly attached to the line!*

Now begin by standing about twice the length of your rod, say twenty feet, from the egg, and try to throw as near to it as you can. We will come to a cast with a fly at the end of it all in good time. All that is wanted at the beginning is the bare line.

At first, you will probably find your line uncommonly hard to manage, to say nothing of hitting the egg with the end of it. But you will very soon discover the first part of the secret, which is… *to give plenty of time for the line to straighten itself out behind you.*

Whenever you hear it make *any* sound, no matter how faint, like the cracking of a whip, you know that you have made your return too quickly.

If you were to do so when it was fitted with a leader and a fly, the chances are that you would pop the fly off altogether. It is hardly necessary to say that there are more profitable ways of spending one's time than in offering to the trout casts with no flies on them.

To get the line out smoothly, you will find that there is also something else required besides avoiding this popping sound: time. That is, by you giving what will at first seem quite an excessive length of time for the line to be located behind you. We will suppose you have got some line out somehow in the direction of the egg, and the point is how to get it back again for another throw.

Don't push yourself too hard at first.

Be content for the first three or four throws with a line only a little longer than the length of your rod. Casting, remember, is almost entirely wrist work, and your wrist needs to be educated to the task.

Well now, let's say we have our line fairly straight out in front of us, what are we to do next? With a turn of the wrist, we bring it back so that it comes over our right shoulder (presuming one is right-handed) between the raised forearm and the face. Then, being always careful to give lots of time for it to uncoil to its fullest extent behind us, we urge it forward.

This time, making it come past the right of the forearm and the rod.

At first, we shall undoubtedly hit ourselves in the face with it when coming back and, with almost equal certainty, tangle it up around the rod when coming forward.

Relax. Be patient. You're learning a new skill, and these things take a little time. This painful phase will probably not last for more than the first quarter to half of an hour.

After that, or sooner, we shall find the line coming neatly and smoothly over our shoulder when it is traveling in one direction—and not touching the rod when it is proceeding in the other direction. Outstanding progress!

Having reached this stage, we shall then reverse the motion, bringing the line *back on the outside* and *forward on the inside.* The idea is to make the line describe a figure rather like a hairpin. And when you come to the water, you will find that it is not only desirable but necessary to be able to do it both ways.

You can pretty much manage it all right now, can you? There you go! I thought you would, for, like many things that appear hard at first glance, casting is pretty straightforward.

Now with each succeeding throw, we will let out a little more line until we have enough to reach the egg, which is still sitting there, looking at us, twenty or even thirty feet away.

Here is where your patience really must prove itself. Because before we go any further, we must be able to hit that egg at least once in every three shots, and never miss it by more than an inch or two.

And, we must be able to do it in every sort of wind—barring a real gale. We shall begin with the wind behind us since that gives us much the most comfortable throw. Then we shall go on to casting across the wind. Finally, we will work to cast directly against the wind, which is a much easier thing to do than you supposed when first you took the rod in hand.

Presently we shall find that we can throw, at any rate, into the near neighborhood of the egg with almost perfect certainty, and that is a significant step gained.

The Next Steps

The next move is, I admit, a bit more difficult. Using the line, we have to hit the egg "as gently," to quote a famous prescription, "as a rose-leaf falling on a lady's veil."

I admit, while not a Labor of Hercules, this is not quite as easy as our work to this point has been.

That is until you grasp the knack of it, and then it is simple enough.

And here's the knack you're looking for: instead of aiming directly at the egg, we aim at a point in the air about two feet above it! Then, when the line is fully extended in the direction of this point, we retard its forward motion with our wrist... and let the line fall on the egg.

Observe most particularly that no part of the line must touch the ground before the end of it is, as it were, hovering over the egg.

So, here we are now: you have learned, in an hour or so's practice, how to cast a line, and now you are naturally eager to have a go with a fly at the end of it.

Do yourself a favor at this juncture.

Wait just a little longer.

By the water, things do *not* arrange themselves quite so conveniently as on a freshly mowed lawn.

On the water, there are trees, branches, rocks, outcrops of stone, bushes, and aggravating clumps of weeds just for a start. Should you, therefore, avoid simulating such circumstances and go about casting your line solely at an egg on your green lawn carpet? Hardly!

In any ordinary front yard or backyard, it is quite easy to imitate many of these difficulties by the straightforward process of—moving the egg into various awkward places. For example, place your trusty target orb slightly behind, say, some ordinary backyard object such as a BBQ, while taking care to make sure the egg is still visible

Or place your casting position with your back to a large tree. Or place the egg in front or to one side of a clump of bushes.

Let your imagination run riot! But—*do not* make the mistake of making the locations for either you or your target egg too hard. It may well sap your enthusiasm for this most rhythmic of water sports. Actually, fly fishing is **all** about rhythm. Finding the right rhythm and movement is the key to casting a fly rod.

Let us presume that some time has now passed, and you feel more confident in your ability to drop your cast line pretty much where you wish.

Congratulations. Well done.

You have learned the beginnings of the management of the line. If you keep at this thing steadily and thoroughly, your rod and your line, in quite a surprisingly brief time, will feel as though it were just an extension of your mind and your right—or left—hand. And when that feeling comes to you, you have gone a very long way on the road to be a competent fly fisher.

Now—you shall fit your line with a leader and with a fly and go to work on that egg in earnest.

> *To be fair, gentle reader, you will find it a good deal more difficult than with the bare line—but do not be discouraged!*

The same principles that got you this far will carry you through this lesson as well. For all that you now need to acquire is… lightness/ suppleness of the hand. Soft, patient, easy-does-it. Let the rod, the fly, and your well-practiced, and now generally fluid technique do the bulk of the work.

> *When, through your backyard practice, you feel you can manage twenty to thirty feet of line and fly, then congratulations: you are quite ready for the waterside. And I promise you that when you get there and begin to cast, you will have no reason to fear the criticism of other anglers.*

At the Water

When you get to the water, your first object must be to keep out of sight of the trout to the degree you can. If dressed conventionally[20], walk slowly or wade whenever and wherever you can. A man standing on the bank in ordinary clothes is clearly visible to every fish within twenty yards of him. In comparison, a man who is wading will hardly be seen at twenty feet.

Alternatively, you can don the latest in UV-safe camouflage clothing and blend in with the background of your locale.

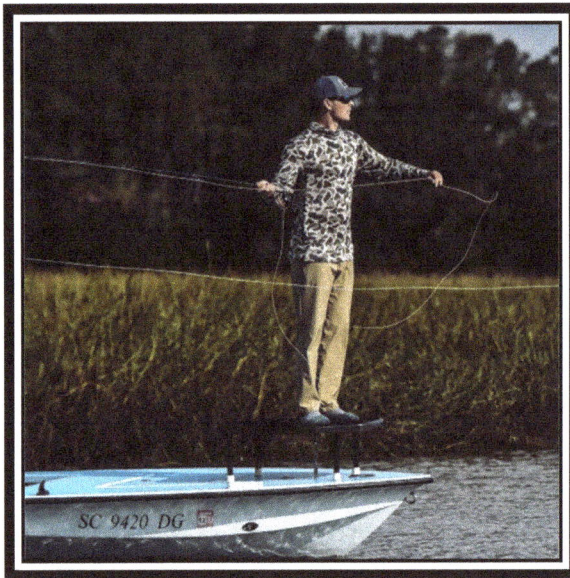

Figure 49 *Note how the pants on this fly fisher generally matches the reeds behind him. And his shirt blends into the tress behind. Even his blue hat "blends" into the sky.*

---

20 **Editor's Note:** *I am presuming you are wearing colors that are "natural" for the environment in which you will be fishing. Browns and greens, maybe some lights blues, rather than loud colors or patterns.*

Bright sunshine and clear water are not ideal conditions, but they are far from hopeless for the angler who wades or camouflages. On such days you will very often see the fish feeding greedily, and you need never despair of getting a decent basket of fish if only you take care to keep out of, or blend into, their sight.

As a broad-based rule, fish upstream (i.e., cast against the flow of the water and not with it) and let the water bring your fly toward you, not carry it away from you. Again, fish almost invariably lie with their heads pointing upstream. And, fortunately for us, even the sharpest-eyed trout is not furnished with eyes in his tail.

RootsRated.com[21] put the "Where do I cast in a stream or river?" subject very succinctly: "Cast around logs, rocks, or the bank, let (the fly) sink a little, and 'strip' (pull) the fly back to you at different speeds to see what works best in that spot. In small streams, look at the other bank and cast your fly upstream at your 3 o'clock position (or 9 o'clock if that's upstream) and let the fly drift until it's all the way down on the other side. Strip it in and repeat. After three attempts, move to a new spot."

Sound advice.

Whatever you do, don't wait for the fly to be carried <u>nearer to you than the point at which you can whisk it neatly off the water</u>. Wait that long, and you are almost sure to get into some sort of difficulty. Again, our friends at RootsRated had some keen advice: "When you are first learning how, fly fish at least 10 feet ahead of where you are, and gradually cast further out. You may see a little rainbow swimming in the far pool but miss the trophy brown trout hiding just behind that rock in front of you."

Capital advice!

So, when you cast again, once the fly has landed (softly!) on the water, let the fly travel a short distance and then take another cast. Doing so now means <u>you can do so comfortably without having to shorten your line</u>. Far and away, the deadliest moment for nailing a fish is that at which the fly first falls (softly!) upon the water—and you can hardly repeat this event too often.

Now is where it gets interesting!

If a fish rises in front of you, *do not throw directly into the circle it has made on the surface of the water.* If you do, it is almost certain to detect the cast line, and the sight of it will alarm it. Instead, cast above and a bit to

---

21 *"So, You Want to Learn How to Fly Fish?", by Charlie Morgan, March 2017 on rootsrated.com.*

one side of it. If done correctly (and softly!), it will see your fly but not your line.

Now, what about if it should rise and refuse?

No sweat. Stay calm. You got this!

Give the fish a minute or so and then come over it again with the same fly, unless you see that there is a rise of something else, in which case change to it.

In either case—*leave this fish alone if it refuses a second time.*

You can bully some fish into taking a fly by repeated throws, but that policy is of no use with a trout. The trout who has twice risen to you and twice refused has made up its mind that there is something suspicious about the affair. As such, it is useless (for you **and** for the trout) to waste any more time. Have you heard the phrase "plenty of fish in the sea"? Well, substitute whatever type of water you are currently working, and the lesson is just as manifest: do not waste time (and patience); move on.

When you get a rise, strike like a flash of lightning—only quicker. The slightest turn of the wrist is enough, but it must be made instantly.

The moment the fish gets your fly in its mouth, it knows it has made a mistake. And, unless it has contrived to hook itself, it will eject it if you give it half a chance to do so.

The art of quick striking is one that can only be acquired by practice, and some people never succeed in mastering it at all. The main thing is to be always on the alert. Constantly. If you find your attention wandering because, perhaps, the fish have not been rising very well for the last half hour or so, stop fishing and sit on the bank until you get keen again. Otherwise, you will simply disturb the water for others and do no good for yourself.

When you have hooked your fish, get on terms with it as quickly as you can. Hold it as tightly as the strength of your tackle will bear and give it no more line than you must.

If it is a good fish, it will give you plenty of trouble anyhow, and you may be sure it knows the whereabouts of every snag in its territory and will do his best to make use of it.

Against a tight line, it cannot do very much, but with a loose one, it is almost sure to get you into some sort of tangle and break you. If it holds on to a water plant with its jaws, as they sometimes will, keep up a steady strain, and it must let go in the end. If it leaps out of the water in the attempt to break your line by falling across it, drop your rod point, and you will foil its move.

Get it below you as soon as you can. First, because you do not want it to disturb the water above you, and, secondly, because when it is below you, you have the power of the stream to help you in fighting it, and can deal with it much more easily.

When it is exhausted, which will be seen by its turning on its side, steer it into a quiet bit of water and get the landing net under it as smoothly as you can. *Even at this moment, beware of a final rush.* A good trout is never caught until it is actually in the net, and the net is <u>out of the water</u>.

Editor's Note

I will leave it to you to decide if you will keep this magnificent animal for your supper or will return it to the wild. When this book was first written, in the mid-1920s, people often had to fish to put any meat on their dinner table. In the 2020s, this is less of an issue by far. I am a steadfast "catch-photograph-and-release" fisher these days. But this issue is for you to decide.

Then get back in the fishing game!

That rise that just yielded your prize could be the only rise of the day! Who can tell? Nothing is more accurate in fly fishing than, as the ancient saying goes, "Fortune and Opportunity are bald behind."

Finally, if you're in a hurry and would instead trade money for time, a decent place to learn how to cast is at your local fly fishing shop. Most big cities (and many moderately sized ones!) have fly fishing shops or an outdoor store with a fly fishing department. Get to know the staff there. These shops often hold no-cost or very inexpensive seminars to learn the essential fly fishing cast.

One last, final word: please be aware of *what is* and *what is not* allowed where you plan to fly fish. Or even if fishing is allowed on that land. (When I was a kid, landowners took many potshots at or near me as an inducement to get off their private (read: posted!) property.) In addition to that, some locations have regulations about what kinds of flies or bait you can use. Nothing ruins a morning of fly fishing more than being thrown off the river accompanied by a $500 fish-and-game bureau fine to pay.

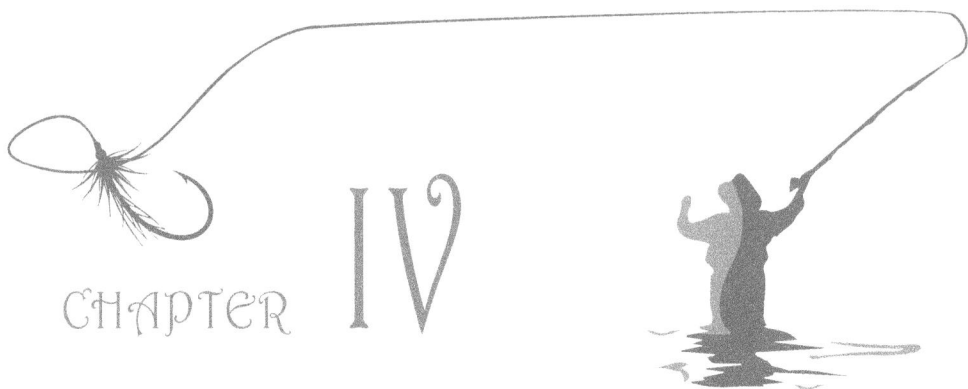

CHAPTER IV

Where to Fish

(1924 edition, edited)

Travel + Leisure magazine said it best: "Until a couple of decades ago, fly fishing meant trying to hook trout. Then the definition of the sport began to expand. Today's fly fisherman is equally intent on landing bonefish in the Bahamas, tarpon in the Florida Keys, Atlantic salmon in eastern Canada, brook and rainbow trout in lower Canada, or Pacific salmon in Alaska.

"It's not surprising that fly fishing has become a near craze, for the sport allows you—no matter how well you can cast, tie a fly, or wade through a rushing stream—intimate contact with some of the most pristine regions of Planet Earth."

Now while the world may well be the ultimate destination for fly fishing, this is an introductory book on the subject. We have to make certain concessions, such as to the probability that you, gentle reader, see your fly fishing in the "trout-and-river/stream" sense rather than fly fishing the northern regions of desolate fjords in Norway.

The novice fly fisher will know adventure if they begin on streams or small rivers in the hills or mountains. I am not going to indicate any particular localities to fish, except to state the obvious: lakes and rivers with known and healthy trout populations should require no introduction, and you should welcome the chance to get to know them all.

But take note, please: if the fly fisher should happen to light upon one of those few-and-far-between paradises in which the trout have not yet eaten of the fruit of the tree of the knowledge of good and evil (i.e.,

the gear, crowds, and bait of your local fly fishing emporium), I strongly advise her or him to keep the fact quiet. Years ago, I found "A Spot" and, like a fool, must need babble and even write about it.

Result: it is now harder work to take two in that water than it used to be to take a dozen.

So, if you please, we will name no names, but confine ourselves to principles.

Now, really, the first and the last of these is to get into the mind of the trout. I will go even further and say that the capacity or the incapacity to do this makes the difference between good and bad in every department of fly fishing. The person destitute of imagination might as well try to write great poetry as to become an accomplished fly fisher.

For the moment, however, we are considering only how to find the fish. To do it, you must ask yourself what sort of a position you would take up if you were a lusty trout bent on picking up a good living with as little exertion as possible.

To begin with, you certainly would *not* station yourself permanently in the main body of, say, a stream where the flow of the water is the most energetic, and the exertion required to "keep station" is the greatest.

If you lived there, it would be because you had not the strength to assert your right to a better place. It is true that now and again, an excellent trout will, for some reason best known to itself, make an expedition into the middle of massive water. When it does, it will tell you so by rising, and you can go for it. But it is only a chance visitor there, for it is not the best place from its point of view, and it is an infallible rule that the best fish hold the best places. If you want them, you must determine which and where the best places are.

Now suppose there is a bit of a rock, or a clump of weed, making a comfortable little backwater with the stream running swiftly on each side of it. That is an ideal spot.

The trout can lie at its ease in the backwater and keep an eye on the food coming down on either side of the rock. If there is an excellent trout in the river, be sure you will find it there.

But—*do not throw into the backwater*. The trout is not accustomed to seeing its meals served in that way. Throw into the stream just above the rock or the clump and trust that the trout will see your fly as it comes past. Seeing that this is what it is used to, you may be sure it is keeping a sharp lookout for flies that go by it in that fashion, and as such, its suspicions will not be aroused.

A deep pool scooped out by the eddies under a bank is always sure to hold good fish.

So is a run between two stones or clumps of weeds when the water is rising. For then the trout are not waiting for the food to come to them, but are on the move looking for it in all the likely places.

In hot, bright weather, they are very fond of lying in the shade of overhanging boughs. If you can put a fly neatly into such a spot, you will often get a good fish when the water is so low and clear that fishing elsewhere is somewhat discouraging.

In the same kind of weather, there will always be two or three sunning themselves in the shallow water at the tail of a pool. But to come over to them with any hope of a rise requires a longish cast, for, as they are close to the surface of the water, they can see the angler a good way off, and will be away into the deep water above at the first alarm.

When the wind is across the stream, fish close to the leeward bank. The flies are naturally blown in that direction, and the trout are perfectly well aware of the fact. If you can manage, without getting hung up, to pitch your fly on to the bank itself and allow the force of the stream, acting on your line, to sweep it unostentatiously into the water, you will nearly always get a rise if there is a trout in the neighborhood. But it is not an easy thing to do without getting into trouble, and it is necessary to prospect carefully for a suitable spot.

Here and there, you will see in the eddies and the tiny backwaters patches of the foam which the country people call "beggar's balm." These are always worth a trial, for the flies become entangled in them, and the trout are on the alert for these mishaps.

Up to the time of the annual feast of the mayfly, the trout tend to frequent slack and shallow-ish waters and to avoid more massive waters. Afterward, being much stronger, they seek them when they are roaming about in search of food.

But the beginning and end of the whole matter is, as I have said, to imagine yourself a trout and ask yourself where, in the particular circumstances of water, weather, and time of year, you would be most likely to take up your position to get <u>the most food with the least amount of trouble and danger.</u>

Success in fly-fishing depends more upon giving an intelligent answer to that question than upon anything else.

Study the water as carefully as a general studies the ground on which (s)he means to fight, and be always on the lookout for every hint that trout give you as to where they are, what they are feeding on, and how, at the moment, they like the dish served.

The only absolute rule is to observe carefully and continuously, and then to draw intelligent conclusions.

Be smart: your prey is.

CHAPTER V

When to Fish

(1924 edition, edited)

THE MAXIM OF A Scottish ancient was: "Aye gang to the watter when the fush are hungry," but I don't know that it helps us very much, for nobody on earth knows what makes the trout rise. Nevertheless, if—and it is a big "if" — you are one of the lucky people who can pick their days, there are a few general rules which may be of some service.

There is almost invariably a rise beginning just very shortly before first light and lasting for about four hours. There is also another which starts in the near dusk/late afternoon and lasts until after dark. These are usually, but by no means invariably, the best fishing times of the day. During these hours, you may expect to get a significant part of your take. But—there are many other subsidiary rises, lasting for half an hour or so, and these it is never safe to neglect. Then again, there is just the luck of a person, a hungry fish, and a well-placed fly! But as a rule, the morning and evening windows yield the best results

Some people pay a great deal of attention to the weather and will not fish on one day because it is too dark and cold, and on another, because it is too bright and hot. As a matter of fact, there is no rule whatever. Broadly speaking, the weather makes extraordinarily little difference. I have had wretchedly miserable days when the weather seemed ideal and outstanding ones when it was, to all appearances, about as discouraging as it could be.

That said, let us have a short word about the wind. The only wind which is worth a button is the one which blows upstream, and, if you get that, the point of the compass from which it comes is of no consequence. Regardless, if dealing with the wind, my recommendation is that should it become vexing enough to turn your mood sour, retire, doff your cap to Mother Nature, and grant her (and the wind) the field of battle for that day. No wind that has ever poorly blown is worth a lousy mood for kith and kin.

As to other weather, you will not get trout with the fly in a torrential flood. When the water is the color of pea-soup, the fish are not troubling about what is happening on the surface. They are fully occupied with the food brought down by the water.

Nor can you expect to do much the day after a flood, for then they are gorged and inert. Also, they seem to know in some mysterious way that a flood is coining some hours before the thick clouds begin to gather. As such, they are apt to cease rising and await the feast that they know is on the way.

Yet, so uncertain are they even in this that I have known them to rise freely in the middle of a massive thunderstorm with the rain coming down in bucket loads.

In fact, the only rule which I have never seen broken is that they will not rise when there is a fog on the surface of the water.

One final somewhat mysterious observation: at some period during almost every day of the season, there is what is called "the time of the take." It may not last for more than an hour, and when it occurs is quite uncertain, except that it is generally before noon. During that hour, or less, every trout in the water will be feeding like an alderperson.

It is then for you to make hay while the sun shines.

The Glossary of Fly Fishing

Reprinted courtesy of Fly Fishers International

Action: An elusive but important characteristic of fly rods. Rods are said to have fast or slow action. Fast action rods are generally stiffer overall, but bend more at the tip, generating higher line speeds and longer casts, especially into the wind. Slow action rods appear to flex their entire length, giving the sense of a more compliant feel.

Albright knot: A common knot used for tying the backing to fly line.

Anadromous: A term to describe fish that travel from the sea upriver to spawn in freshwater like salmon. Fish that migrate from freshwater to the sea for spawning are catadromous.

Angler: One who seeks to catch fish with a hook (an "angle"), usually fixed to the end of a line.

Anti-Reverse: A feature of fly reels where the spool handle does not turn as the line is pulled out from the reel.

Attractor: A style or variety of fly that is effective in eliciting strikes, but has few apparent characteristics of a natural food item. Often an attractor is flashy and bigger than life.

Arbor: The center part of a fly reel where line and backing (first) is wound.

Arbor knot: A knot used for tying backing to the arbor of the fly reel.

Back cast: The casting of the line in a direction opposite to the direction the fly is intended to go. The backward counterpart of the forward cast, which acts to create a bending action on the fly rod, setting up the conditions to generate the forward cast and present the fly.

Backing: The first segment of line on a reel, usually braided and used to build up the arbor and to offer additional distance for a strong fish to pull out line. An unusually strong fish will take you "into your backing."

Badger: A feather of a specially bred or chosen chicken that has colors that change from brown-black to black at the center of the quill to ginger or white on the outer edges.

Barbless: Barbless hooks are either manufactured without a barb, or the barb is squeezed down. This feature makes it easier to remove a hook and minimizes the handling and potential damage of a fish you may want to release.

Barrel knot: See blood knot.

Beadhead: Usually, but not always, a fly with a bead immediately behind the hook eye. Beads come in many materials, from brass to nickel-brass to ceramic. Some beads help a fly sink, but others are floaters.

Belly: A tapered fly line has several components, with a relatively sharply tapered tip (at the fly end). The middle portion of the line is called the belly.

Belly boat: Originally using a tractor or truck inner tube, this is a one-person craft with a seat across the bottom on which the fly fisher sits. Feet are in the water, and scuba fins are used to move the tube around. This type of fishing boat is very popular with warm water fly fishers and with individuals who fish high mountain lakes. Also called a "belly boat." *See Kick boat.*

Bimini twist: A knot used in saltwater fly fishing say for tarpon. It has a loop and a double line section making it exceptionally strong.

Blank: Fiberglass and graphic fly rods (which also have fiberglass) are produced by wrapping sheets of graphite and fiberglass around a carefully tapered steel rod (called a mandrel). The hollow rod that results from this process is called a blank. It has no guides, ferrules, or reel seat.

Blood knot: A best known for its strength in tying monofilaments of different diameter and material together. It is rather difficult to tie on the water, and commercially made blood knot tiers are available to make the job easier. A blood knot is often used to create a fly leader of several different diameter monofilament segments. Also known as a barrel knot.

Bobbin: A fly tying tool and term borrowed from sewists. A bobbin holds the tying thread.

Bodkin: A bodkin is a tool best described as a needle with a handle. It can be easily made from a piece of wooden doweling and a needle. It is used in fly tying used to deposit cement or lacquer to a fly.

Braided loop connector: A way of putting an in-line loop at the end of your fly line to use the loop on the leader to make a loop-to-loop connection between the leader and the fly line. The braided loop connector works like the so-called "Chinese finger torture."

Breakoff: A term of defeat and excitement for a fly angler describing the event of a hooked fish breaking your tippet or leader. Usually, a breakoff results from an unusually strong or big fish.

Bucktail: A streamer fly tied to imitate a fish. This fly usually features a long segment of hair, laid back from the eye to the bend of the hook. That hair often is from a deer's tail.

Butt section: The thicker end of a tapered leader that is tied to the fly line.

Caddis: A common aquatic insect found in many streams and rivers. They are a favorite food of trout and other fish. They have some distinct stages, including an underwater pupa and an above the water surface adult. Caddis have tent-shaped wings and are known in both lakes and rivers to fly down upon the water to deposit their eggs.

Catch and release: A practice originating in the late 1930s to conserve fish populations by unhooking and returning a caught fish to the water in which it was caught. This is a highly successful practice in many warm water, cold water, and saltwater settings.

Caudal fin: Caudal is an anatomical term meaning "the back." The caudal fin is the tail fin or tail of a fish.

Char: A species of fish that is related to trout, that prefers cold water and is found many places in the world, including both east and west United States. Examples of char are brook trout, lake trout, arctic char, and Dolly Varden.

Click drag: A mechanical system on many inexpensive fly reels used to slow down or resist the pulling efforts of a fish, to slow the fish down and tire it to the point where it can be landed. A clicking sound is created by a triangular steel ratchet snaps over the teeth of the gear in the reel spool. The term singing reels refers to the high-frequency clicking associated with a big fish pulling out line.

Clinch knot: A very popular knot for tying the tippet to the fly. It has the advantage of being very easy to tie and not use much line. *See Improved Clinch.*

Collar: A ring of feathers or hair placed immediately behind the head of the fly.

Curve cast: A casting technique that allows an angler to cast a fly around an obstacle. It is also used to minimize the influence of water current or wind on the fly or the fly line.

Dapping: A relatively ancient technique of presenting a fly on the surface of the water where the fly is connected to a short piece of line on a long rod. The fly is then touched on the surface of the water, immediately over a place where a fish might lie.

Dead drift: A term applied to the way that artificial flies must drift with the current to appear natural. This requires that the fly line, leader and tippet move with the fly and cause unnatural drag or a "v" that will result in most fish refusing the fly.

Disk drag: A mechanical system on more expensive fly reels whereby resistance is created to the line as a fish pulls it out. This resistance is intended to slow the fish and tire it. The resistance proper is created by applying pressure between two disks. Different from the click drag, the disk drag is smoother and less likely to create a sudden force that will break the line

Double haul: The term for the cast where the caster quickly pulls and releases the line on both the back cast and the forward cast. It is used to create greater line speed, enabling the caster to reach farther or cut through wind.

Double taper: DT or double taper refers to a fly line that is reduced in diameter on both ends. When one end of a DT fly line wears out, you can take it off the reel, turn it around, and use the other end.

Drag: This term has two meanings in fly fishing: (1) An unnatural pulling of a floating or submerged fly such that it moves at a different rate than the current, often (at least on the surface) creating a "V" in the water—fish are commonly put off by drag. (2) A mechanical system that is part of a fly reel to resist and slow the speed at which line is pulled off the reel by a hooked fish.

Dropper: A practice of fishing two flies at the same time, often one on the surface and a second underwater. This increases the chances of getting a successful fly in front of a fish.

Dry fly: A fly constructed of water resistant, lightweight, and buoyant materials so as to imitate an insect that alights or floats on the surface of the water.

Dubbing: Fly tying material (usually strands or fibrous, including fur, yarn, wool, or synthetic fibers) that are wrapped onto a thread (commonly using wax) and wrapped around the shank of the hook to imitate the abdomen and/or thorax of an artificial fly.

Duncan's loop: A monofilament knot used most often to tie a tippet to the eye of a hook. Also called a uni-knot.

Dun: This word has two related uses in fly fishing: (1) a grayish or grayish blue (dull) color often seen in the wings of mayfly adults, (2) an aquatic insect in a life stage just as it has emerged from the water and can fly.

Emerger: A term for an aquatic insect at the stage when it swims to the surface or just below the surface to hatch or change from a nymph or pupa to a winged adult.

False cast: Casting the fly line forward and back in the air as a means to lengthen the amount of line that extends out from the rod, to dry the fly or to modify the path of the line. In a false cast, the fly is not allowed to drop onto the water.

Ferrule: A collar that is found at the point where sections of a fly rod are joined. The end of one section fits inside the end of another, in an overlapping fashion at the ferrule.

Flat: An expansive area of water with a relatively unchanging (flat) depth, often over a sand or grass bottom. A common water topography for certain species of fish, like bonefish.

Floatant: A water-proofing (usually oily) salve or cream that is used to help flies, leaders, and fly lines float.

Float tube: Originally using a tractor or truck inner tube, this is a one-person craft with a seat across the bottom on which the fly fisher sits. Feet are in the water and scuba fins are used to move the tube around. This type of fishing boat is very popular with warmwater fly fishers and with individuals who fish high mountain lakes. *See kick boat.*

Fly: An imitation of a fish food item, traditionally very light and made of hair, feathers, and thread tied to a hook. Modern flies have many synthetic materials and often include lead to help them sink.

Fly fishing: A technique for fishing where the weight of the line is used to cast a very light weight fly that would not be heavy enough to be cast with a conventional spinning or casting rod.

Fly line: A line for fly fishing, originally of silk but currently made of a plastic coating over a braided line core. Fly lines are commonly 1.5 to 2 mm in diameter. The plastic coating gives the line weight and is commonly distributed unevenly to make the line easier to cast. A weight forward line, for example, has a greater plastic thickness near the forward (or fly) end of the line. Fly lines are not particularly long, generally not exceeding 105 feet. See taper, weight forward, double taper. Fly lines are rated in different weights, from 1 to 11, referring to the weight of the first 30 feet of the fly line.

Fly reel: A special fishing reel with fairly simple mechanics (compared to spinning or bait casting reels) designed to hold large diameter fly line.

A fly reel is relatively light and attaches below the handle on a fly rod. More sophisticated (and expensive) fly reels have a drag system that creates resistance to the rapid pulling off of line by a fish. See drag, click drag, disk drag.

Fly rod: The special fishing rod constructed so as to cast a fly line. Fly rods are generally longer and thinner than spinning or casting rods. The special design involves careful attention to the way the fly rod bends because that bending action determines how well it can help cast a fly line. Fly rods were originally split cane bamboo. In the last 60 years, other materials, especially fiberglass and fiberglass with embedded graphite fibers are used. Fly rods are rated in their stiffness to match fly lines of different weights. (a number 6 fly rod should be used with a number 6 fly line). *See fly lines.*

Freestone stream: A creek or river that gets most of its water flow from rainfall or snow/glacier melt. Freestone streams are most common in mountainous regions. The name freestone refers to the fact that typical freestone streams have a bottom of stones or gravel.

Fry: The first stage of a fish after hatching from an egg.

Forceps: A special medical pliers with a ratchet-locking action that are useful in removing a hook from a fish. These slim-nosed pliers are readily available in a number of lengths and sizes. Check a local medical supply.

Furnace: The coloration of feathers from a specially bred chicken that are dark brown to black along the center changing to light browns on the edge.

Gaiters: Commonly a neoprene anklet or legging put over the top of wading shoes and to keep gravel from getting into the shoe and abrading the stocking foot of the wader. These are also called gravel guards.

Ghillie: A fishing guide in Britain, especially in Scotland, Wales, and Ireland, where the term originates from the Celts.

Graphite: A common material which if formed into fibers and placed in the fiber glass of a fly rod, makes the rod relatively stiff with little increase in weight as compared to fiber glass alone.

Grilse: A young, not sexually mature Atlantic salmon.

Grip: The cork handle of a fly rod, generally made of cork rings shaped in several different ways, including a cigar grip, full-wells grip, half-wells grip, and superfine grip.

Grizzly: The coloration pattern from a specially bred chicken with barred black and white "V" pattern. Very popular for many flies because it may create the illusion of motion.

Guide: Metal rings, usually bent pieces of wire along the length of the fly rod to ease the release of line during casting and to distribute the stress of a fish along the entire length of the rod.

Hackle: Feathers from the neck or back of a specially bred chicken that are wrapped around the hook or otherwise attached to a fly to imitate parts of an insect, such as legs or segments of the body. Hackle tips are used also for the wings on certain flies.

Hackle gauge: A ruler-like device to make sure the length of hackle used is appropriate for the size of hook. Particularly, hackle feather fibers (barbules) on a classic dry fly should be the same length as the hook gap.

Hackle pliers: Pliers used to hold feathers while they are being wound around a hook. Generally hackle pliers are spring loaded and often have a rubber disk to hold the slippery feathers.

Hairbug: A fly constructed through a special technique called hair spinning whereby buoyant (hollow) winter-coat, slippery deer, elk, antelope, or caribou hair is made to flare and form a solid shape. This hair can be further trimmed to shapes like frog bodies. Hairbugs are commonly used for warmwater fish, but a mouse imitation hairbug is excellent for big brown trout on certain waters.

Hair stacker: A cylinder with one end blocked that is used to get tips of animal hair lined up for wings, tails, and other parts of a fly. A spent rifle cartridge is suitable for small bunches of hair.

Hatch: Generally refers to a stage of aquatic insect change when there is a transformation from a swimming to a fly stage and from an underwater to a surface stage. Insects in the early part of this transition are also referred to as emergers.

Haul: A pull on the fly line with the non-casting hand to increase the line speed and get greater distance. This is done effectively during line pickup. An action associated with fly casting whereby the line speed is increased with an extra pull during line pickup, or back casting. *See double haul.*

Hook size: To a degree hooks are standardized based upon the gap (or gape) which is defined as the distance between the hook shank and the hook point. Smaller numbers refer to larger hooks, consistent with the origin of hooks made from steel wire stock. Hooks for fly fishing range from a very small #24 (gap of 2 mm) to very large #2 (hook gap of 10 mm).

Improved clinch knot: A popular knot to tie a monofilament tippet to the eye of a hook. Also called the Trilene knot, after substantial publicity by the folks at Berkeley. If the tippet is run through the loop twice it is even stronger.

Keeper: A loop of thin wire built into the shaft of the fly rod (near the grip) the fly can be attached while still connected to the tippet and line. This allows the fly fisher freedom to walk and climb without concern about hooking trees, grass, or himself.

Kype: A male spawning trout or salmon develops a hook-like protrusion on the mandible. The kype is particularly striking in salmon.

Leader: A single piece of tapered monofilament or multiple segments of monofilament stepped down from large where it is attached to the fly line to small where it is attached to the tippet. The butt end is usually fairly large and stiff (say 0.023 inches diameter) with the tippet end around 3X or 4X (.008-.007 inches). The section near the fly may include a tippet.

Lie: Areas in a river or lake where fish hang out, commonly well-located because they are out of the main current, present cover from predators, or provide a good source of insects and other food.

Line dressing: An old term carried over from the days of silk fly lines referring to the oily substances applied to clean and increase buoyancy. Modern fly lines generally only need to be cleaned with warm water and soap.

Line weight: The weight of the first 30 feet of a fly line, used as a way to standardize fly lines in matching them to fly rods of differing stiffness. Line weighting is not a linear numbering system; the first 30 feet of a #6 weight line 160 grains while the first 30 feet of a #3 weight line is 100 grains.

Loading: A term used to describe the effect of the weight of the line and the momentum of the cast upon the rod. A loaded rod is bent or loaded more with a greater casting force and a heavier line.

Loop to loop: A way to connect a fly line and a leader by making a loop at the end of the leader (perfection loop knot) and a loop attached to the end of the fly line. Loop to loop connections are sometimes made from a leader to a tippet.

Marabou: Fluffy and soft down or underfeathers from most birds, but particularly for fly tying, marabou comes from chickens, turkeys, or other domestic fowl.

Matching the hatch: An attempt by a fly angler to select an artificial fly that imitates the color, size, shape, and behavior of natural insects that fish are feeding on at a particular time. Often when a hatch is happening, fish become very selective and refuse insects that are not the most abundant.

Mayfly: An aquatic insect found throughout the world, in both still water and rivers. It is most easily identified by its sail-like upright wings and long graceful tails. Many classic trout flies imitate mayflies. Mayflies vary in size from the 3 mm tricos to the 30 mm hexagenia.

Mend: Throwing an upstream curve into your fly line as it floats down the stream to avoid having water currents pull on it and cause unnatural movement of your fly (unnatural drift or line drag). Fish and especially trout are exquisitely sensitive to (and turned off by) movement of an insect that moves at a different rate or in a different direction than the current.

Midge: A very small (non-biting), two-winged insect, related to deer flies, mosquitos, and crane flies.

Monofilament: A single filament or strand of nylon, primarily used for tippet material or, if tapered, for leaders.

Nail knot: A knot tied with a nail as a prop and often used to attach the fly line to the backing. Also used less commonly to tie the leader to the fly line. Also called a tube knot.

Nymph: An underwater stage of aquatic insect. It is an important source for all varieties of warmwater and cold-water fish.

Palmered: A term used to describe feathers wound perpendicular to the shank of the hook and apparently based upon appearance of pilgrims bearing palms.

Parachute style fly: A dry fly with the dry fly hackle wrapped horizontally under the hook or at the base of the wings, providing a type of outrigger flotation.

Parr: A young trout, salmon or char, usually in the so-called fingerling stage.

Perfection loop: This is a knot often used to create a loop in a piece of monofilament, frequently at the butt end of a leader for the loop to loop connection.

Polarized sunglasses: Sunglasses with iodized lenses that block incident light (glare) and thus allow anglers to better see beneath the surface glare of water.

Pool: A reach or segment of a river or stream with greater depth and slower current, making it safer from predators, birds, and animals and where swimming against the current is reduced.

Popper: A topwater lure, made of painted balsa wood or deer hair, with a flat face that causes it to make a popping sound when retrieved. It is commonly used for warmwater panfish, bass, and some saltwater species.

Presentation: A term referring to the placing of a fly to the feeding region of a fish. While it appears to be a pretentious term, it reflects the precision and elegance of casting a fly in a manner that it perfectly imitates a natural insect.

Pupa: An intermediate stage of certain insects, generally the stage between the larva and adult form of caddis flies or midges. Also refers to the fly imitation of these insects.

Reach cast: A cast used for adding extra slack in the line, or when fishing downstream, in order to provide a more natural float.

Reel seat: The section of a fly rod below the grip where the fly reel is attached. Reel seats often are constructed of attractive wood, including many exotic woods.

Redd: The hollowed out nest in a streambed where a fish deposits its eggs, a behavior typical to most salmonids.

Reel seat: The part of the fly rod—made of aluminum, wood, or graphite and located just behind the grip—where the fly reel is attached.

Retrieve: The method of stripping in the fly line that gives the fly action. Also, a term used in describing fly reels, as to whether they are left hand or right hand retrieve.

Rise: The action of a fish as it comes to the surface of the water to feed. Different kinds of rises (splashy, dimpled, etc.) suggest different kinds of feeding and may suggest different kinds of insects.

Roll cast: This is a casting technique that is used when a back cast is not possible. The line is made to loop in front of the angler and if properly executed it "rolls" out to present the fly.

Run: This term has two meanings in fly fishing: (1) A section of stream where relatively shallow water goes over a rough or gravel bottom and then into a pool. (2) The pulling out of line a hooked fish makes in trying to escape.

Running line: A thin line made of monofilament, Dacron braid, or thin fly line that connects on one end to a shooting head and on the other end to the backing and indirectly the reel.

Scud: A small freshwater scrimp-like crustacean that is present in most trout waters and serves as a food source for trout.

Sea-run: A term describing brown, cutthroat, and rainbow trout that hatch in fresh water, migrate to the sea to mature, and return to fresh water to spawn. Rainbow trout (in the Pacific Northwest and Great Lakes) are the best known sea-run trout; these are called steelhead.

Setting the hook: To make sure the hook penetrates the fish's mouth, an angler must apply an upward motion of the fly rod or some sort of quick tension on the fly line. When fishing with artificial lures and flies, fish often do not hook themselves because very soon after they "mouth" the fly, they are aware that it does not feel, taste, or smell like it should. They will spit it out! This puts a premium on setting the hook at the right time!

Shooting head: Part of a special fly line used for long distance casting. The shooting head is a heavy section of line attached to a thin running line (made of monofilament, Dacron, or fine fly line). The shooting head has almost all of the weight of a normal line, but obviously is it almost totally concentrated in that first 30 feet. Shooting heads are used for making long casts in fishing saltwater, warmwater, and steelhead.

Shooting line: The process of extending the length of your fly cast by releasing an extra length of fly line (usually held in your non-casting hand) during the forward/presentation part of the cast. This technique allows a fly angler to false cast a shorter segment of line and then only at the time of the final forward cast to bring a longer segment of line into play.

Single action: The typical fly reel wherein a single turn of the handle causes one turn of the reel spool. This is distinguished from the multiplier reel where a single turn of the handle causes multiple turns of the spool and makes it easier to retrieve line. Almost all high quality fly reels are single action.

Sink Tip: A fly line that has both a floating segment (say the first 95 feet) and a sinking section (the last 10 feet). This style of line is used for underwater presentation of flies in fast water or in some still water fishing situations.

Spawn: The behavior of fish where females deposit eggs (also called spawn) on various surfaces (varying with species) and the male produces necessary milt to ultimately turn the eggs into fry.

Spey: A particular casting technique using special two-handed rods and a modified roll cast. It is named after the river in Scotland where it was developed.

Split cane rods: Fly rods constructed of six pieces of split cane bamboo, which are triangularly shaped, tapered, and glued together. Split cane rods appear to have originated in the U.S. in the middle of the 19th century. While used by some modern anglers, graphite/fiber glass rods offer less expensive and easier-to-care-for options.

Spinner: The last stage of a mayfly, based upon the fact that the wings are spread horizontally as it falls to water surface after mating. The spinner is of significance because the spinner is an easy target for feeding fish.

Spinner fall: When mayflies of a particular sub-species go into the spinner stage they do so over a relatively short period of time, sometimes creating a feeding frenzy during what is called a spinner fall.

Spring creek: A creek or stream that gets its water from a ground flow or spring sources, rather than glacier/snow melt or surface run-off. Spring creeks are generally at a temperature of the average rainfall temperature over the course of the year (the source of most ground water) and hence usually do not warm significantly in the summer nor freeze in the winter.

S-cast: An "S" pattern of the fly line on the water created by side-to-side movement of the fly rod during the forward cast. This cast is used to put slack in the fly line and hence to reduce the influence of the current on the fly line and thus to minimize drag.

Stonefly: An aquatic insect found throughout North America that generally requires higher water quality than most fish, including trout. It varies in size, but in the larger sub-species can reach 2 inches. Its life stages vary from mayflies and caddis flies inasmuch as it crawls out of the water onto a rock, splits its outer covering, and becomes a flying insect with wings that lie on its back.

Streamer: A fly classically made of long soft feathers or animal hair (like bucktail) to imitate a bait fish, leech, or other non-insect. Modern streamers are made of many synthetic materials, including metallic film and even epoxy.

Strike: The action of a fish in trying to eat a fly. This term also refers to the movement of the rod a fly angler makes to set the hook.

Stripping guide: The guide nearest the reel on a fly rod, usually more substantial and larger in diameter than the snake guides nearer the tip. It is called a stripping guide because in bringing in the fly, the line is pulled over this guide with a fair amount of force. Some rods have two stripping guides, with the larger being nearer the reel.

Surgeon's knot: A common and strong knot for tying tippet material to the leader or one segment of tippet material to another. A surgeon's knot is stronger than a blood knot, especially for connecting materials of unlike size and material. The blood knot has the advantage of being smoother and less likely to catch algae or cause tangles.

Steelhead: A variety of rainbow trout that spawns and lives part of its life in freshwater streams and other parts in oceans. While native to the Pacific Ocean, steelhead have been successfully introduced into many large lakes and now are found in some tributaries of all of North America's Great Lakes.

Stripping: Bringing in a fly line with a series of short or varied pulls so as to simulate a living insect or bait fish. Often also involves movements of the rod tip.

Tail out: The lower end of a pool where it becomes shallow again.

Tailing: This term refers to the behavior of fish in shallow water where it is possible to see the caudal fins as they feed. Tailing fish are an exciting discovery and generally signal the possibility of getting strikes by the proper presentation of the right fly.

Tailwater: The downstream section of a river or stream found below a large man-made dam. The most famous and productive tailwaters are from bottom-discharge dams, making the water relatively cold and constant in temperature.

Terrestrial insect: As the name implies, these are land-dwelling (or tree/plant-dwelling) insects that breath air, including grasshoppers, crickets, ants, beetles, and leaf worms.

Tinsel: A thin silver, gold, or brass-colored ribbon used in adding shine to flies, often as ribbing or for fly bodies.

Tippet: The terminal segment of monofilament tied on the end of a leader and connected to the fly.

Tip section: The top section of a fly rod, smallest in diameter and furthest from the rod grip.

Tip-top: A guide for the fly line with a small cylinder attached that fits over the end of the fly rod.

Triangle taper: A special taper profile to a fly line designed by Lee Wulff, with 40 feet of continuous taper, with a thin running line. Particularly useful for roll casts.

Variant: A dry fly variety of wound hackles that are much larger than normally recommended. It is tied generally the same as conventional patterns.

Vise: A tool used by fly tiers to hold the hook secure as thread, feathers, and fur are attached and the fly is being constructed. Usually the most expensive and the single most important purchase for a fly tier.

Wader belt: An adjustable belt cinched near the top of chest waders to keep out water, particularly recommended as a precaution to the waders filling up with water in the event of a fall.

Waders: Footed trousers that are constructed of latex, neoprene, Gortex, or other waterproof material so as to keep anglers dry. Currently waders come in stocking foot or booted form and can be found in three lengths: hip waders, waist-high waders, and chest waders.

Wading shoes or boots: Hiking-like boots worn with stocking foot waders, generally having felt soles and a more comfortable fit than the boot portions of boot foot waders.

Wading staff: A walking stick especially adapted to provide stability to a wading fly angler when moving through fast or deep water. Some wading staffs are foldable and can be kept in a fishing vest pocket until needed.

Weedguard: A piece of stiff monofilament or light wire attached from the top of the hook and extending in front of the hook point and bend to the hook eye. If properly attached, a weedguard reduces the likelihood of a fly picking up weeds, yet it does not deter the hooking of a fish. Weedguards are especially popular for underwater warmwater flies.

Weight forward: A type of fly line with most of its weight in the first thirty feet of line. The large section of this type of line is called the line belly, with a long tapering of the line toward the front and a short tapering of it back to a thinner running line.

Wet fly: A type of fly that is presented to the fish below the surface of the water, usually with insect-like wings sloped backward. Wet flies are not as popular as they once were and have been largely superseded by nymphs.

Whip finisher: A tool used in tying flies that helps the fly tier lay down a smooth and compact head of the fly.

Winding: Wraps of thread that are used to attach the stripping guides and snake guides on the fly rod blank.

Wind knots: In the process of casting, especially for beginners, loops form particularly in the leader and tippet. The formation of such loops is made worse by casting in the wind, and hence when they become knots in the leader or tippet they are called wind knots.

X diameter: A system to indicate the diameter of leader and tippet material, with 0X (zero-X) representing the largest diameter (.011 inches) and 8X (.003 inches) representing a small, light diameter. Commonly used values are 1X (.010), 2X (.009), 3X (.008), 4X (.007), 5X (.006), and 6X (.005). The strength of these monofilament diameters varies with the kind of material.

~ The End ~

www.ingramcontent.com/pod-product-compliance
Lightning Source LLC
Chambersburg PA
CBHW041215030426
42336CB00023B/3353